Bold as Fuck

Bold Voices
The Truth and Chaos of Real Entrepreneurship

Volume Three

NICOLA PEAKE

Published in 2025 by Discover Your Bounce Publishing

www.discoveryourbouncepublishing.com

Copyright © Discover Your Bounce Publishing

All rights reserved.
Printed in the United States of America & the UK. No part of this book may be used, replicated or reproduced, stored in a retrieval system, or transmitted in any form or by any means, electronic, mechanical, photocopying, recording, or otherwise, without the written permission of the author(s). Quotations of no more than 25 words are permitted, but only if used solely for the purposes of critical articles or reviews.

ISBN 978-1-914428-45-6

Although the author and publisher have made every effort to ensure that the information in this book is correct at the time of going to print, the author and publisher do not assume and therefore disclaim liability to any party. The author and the publisher will not be held responsible for any loss or damage save for that caused by their negligence.

Although the author and the publisher have made every reasonable attempt to achieve accuracy in the content of this book, they assume no responsibility for errors or omissions.

Page design and typesetting by Discover Your Bounce Publishing

"The key is to keep going. Ask for support when you need it. You don't have to do it alone."

Sara Davies

CONTENTS

FOREWORD BY NICKY MARSHALL………………..….…..	1
INTRODUCTION BY NICOLA PEAKE…………………...	4
CLAIRE HUGGINS………………………………………..	6
A Little Girl's Dream……………………………………....….	7
FIONA FORSTER……………………………………………...	19
Feel the Fire but do it Anyway…………………………….…..	20
JO SHELTON……………………………………….………...	31
The Rebirth of a Woman Who Refused to Stay Invisible…………..	32
MIKE CALDER……………………………………………...	42
Wild Purpose……………………………………………...….	43
NICOLA PEAKE……………………………………...………	55
The 'Bold as Fuck' Come Back…………………………….….	56
SARA SOUTHEY……………………………………...……..	70
Speak Up! I Can't Hear You…………………….………….....	71
SHANE EVANS……………………………………………...	82
Drifting to Driving……………………………………….…..	83

SHARON BANHAM………………………..………….. 95

Unlock the Courage to be Seen…………………………….…... 96

WORK WITH NICOLA…………………………...……….. 107

ACKNOWLEDGMENTS

Writing a book like this takes effort and there are lots of people that made this happen! Firstly, to my amazing 'Bold as Fuck' authors, thank you for being brave and getting your message out there!

Thanks to the team at Discover Your Bounce Publishing and Mark from Brand 51 for another cool cover.

Finally, thanks to you, for buying this book!

FOREWORD
By Nicky Marshall

I love watching the human spirit in action. As people we go through life experiencing the good, the bad and everything in between. Sometimes life can be wonderful, and heart breaking at exactly the same time. We can feel on top of the world, and then crushed. Yet still we get up, dust ourselves off and go again.

As entrepreneurs, we put this human spirit on show. We create a business, we nurture it and love it and then parade it in the world asking, "Do you like what I've created?" At times when we are uncertain, or tired, or working through life challenges we still put this part of ourselves on parade. We ask people to trust us, to put faith in our dream, to come with us on the journey.

And sometimes we get it wrong.

As an entrepreneur myself I've got it wrong. I've had to close businesses, walk away from partnerships and face my loved ones and share my failures. It hurts. There are dark nights of the soul and lots of self-interrogation…'what could I have done differently?' After a while though, there is a new spark. A renewed strength, more passion and the knowledge that we have something that could do some good in the world. I am thankful that I kept going, as today I have three thriving businesses and a business partner that makes my heart sing.

When I first met Nicola Peake, I knew she was an entrepreneur. I could see that passion, her zest for bringing her ideas to life - and she has a lot of ideas! I watched as she brought business owners together and created the spaces to help them flourish. I also admired how openly she shared when she got it wrong. How she held her head above the criticism in the online space and set about rising again. I could see her hurt, but I could also see that spark that refused to be diminished.

They call entrepreneurship The Heroes Journey. Entrepreneurs don't feel like heroes most of the time. They work tirelessly, spend hours that others wouldn't, in the hope of creating a lifestyle that others can't. They question their actions; they toil over the details and have a mission to help others through their offerings.

In this book you will hear stories from heroes. People who have faced adversity, who have dug deep and battled through. In these pages there are nuggets of gold, wisdom to be learned and a trail of breadcrumbs for you if you are ready for more; to rise again.

Every author has shared their vulnerability, been open about their uncertainty and written their story in the hope that you, our reader, can live a life of your choosing. Not in a quiet, apologetic way that lives in the mediocre but in a way that is bold. A life on your terms, however that looks in your dreams and vision. To be seen, to be heard, to know that your voice matters. To know that way you think and what you do is important.

Bold as f*ck.

INTRODUCTION

There's a moment in every business where you wonder what the hell you're doing. When everything you've worked for feels shaky, when your confidence dips, when you start questioning if you've got what it takes. We've all been there. Every single one of us.

This book was created to remind you that you're not alone.

Inside these pages, eight bold voices share their stories — the real ones. The highs, the heartbreaks, the breakthroughs, and the moments that changed everything. Each chapter is different because every journey is. But what connects them all is courage. The courage to keep going when things felt heavy. The courage to start again. The courage to stay bold when it would have been easier to hide.

Being Bold As F*ck isn't about being loud, confident, or fearless all the time. It's about showing up anyway. It's about falling, crying, screaming, and then getting back up, fixing your crown, and taking the next step forward. It's messy, it's emotional, it's real — but it's where the magic happens.

Whether you're at the top of your game or rebuilding from the ground up, this book will remind you that boldness isn't something you find, it's something you choose. Every day.

So grab a drink, get comfy, and let these stories remind you that the messy middle is where the best things are born. Because being Bold As F*ck doesn't mean you never fall. It means you always rise.

Nicola Peake

Claire Huggins

I'm Claire Huggins, Founder and Creative Director of Claire Louise Branding a luxury design studio crafting bold, iconic brands for visionary leaders and entrepreneurs. With over 20 years of experience in design and advertising, and an RSA Award for creativity, I combine strategy, intuition, and artistry to build brands that radiate confidence and clarity. Through my work, I help businesses evolve their visual identity, elevate their authority, and lead with distinction. I also host Mastermind Days, guiding others to embody their next level of brand presence.

Connect with me:
Facebook @clairelouisebranding
Instagram @clairelouisebranding
LinkedIn @clairehuggins
or visit www.clairelouisebranding.co.uk

A Little Girl's Dream: From Rock Bottom to Bold as Fuck

It's 5am on a Monday morning. The house is quiet, my coffee is strong, and I'm sitting here thinking about how far I've come. Not because the road has been easy. Quite the opposite. I've had to fight for every single part of the life I have today.

This isn't just about my business. This is my story.

A fucking remarkable story.

And if there's one thing I know about women, it's that we don't stop, nearly enough, to celebrate; how far we've come, how much we've survived, and how much we've built from scratch.

I'm writing this as a widow. A mum of three to Sophie, 22, Chloe, 15, and George, 7. A proud nanny to my gorgeous grandson, Jace. A daughter, a sister, a sister-in-law, a niece, a daughter-in-law, a friend, and a girlfriend.

I wear many hats. Some I chose. Some life gave me whether I wanted them or not.

The past few years have been some of the most challenging of my life. There have been moments where life knocked me flat, but there have also been moments of joy, growth and empowerment. Honestly, my story could fill a Netflix series.

The Little Girl Who Dreamed Big

My love for design started as a little girl sitting in my bedroom. I'd spend Sundays recording the Top 40 on cassette tapes, flicking through *Smash Hits* magazine, surrounded by posters of Madonna, New Kids on the Block and A-ha. I can still see myself copying Madonna's *True Blue* album cover, imagining that one day I'd be a designer.

My parents, Anne and Stephen always supported me. They never got in the way of my dreams. Dad, a sergeant in the Metropolitan Police, raised me to be strong, to stand my ground and hold my own. Mum was a nurse from Ireland, and her own story could be a book. She grew up as an orphan, and those early days were incredibly tough, but she built a life from nothing. She was resilient, compassionate, and endlessly creative.

I know I get my strength from both, my mum's resilience and compassion, my dad's grit and determination. From Mum, I learned to care deeply and create beauty even from difficult beginnings. From Dad, I learned to stand my ground and keep moving forward no matter what. Together they taught me that no dream was too big if I was willing to work for it.

I wasn't naturally academic at school. I had to work harder than most of my friends to get the grades I needed, but I loved art and business studies. When I achieved the results to go on and study a BTEC in Art and Design, I was so proud and so were my parents.

I still remember driving back from our holiday in Norfolk to get my

GCSE results. My dad was there with me, standing by my side as I opened that envelope. Then he drove us all the way back to our holiday, because the long drive was nothing for the daughter he loved and the family he dedicated his life to.

To pay my way I stacked shelves in a supermarket, worked eight years at Ravel shoe shop where my love of shoes began and later worked at Morgan, a French fashion brand I adored.

Then came my next big step: studying HND Graphic Design at Amersham and Wycombe College. From day one I knew I was in the right place. It was clear this was a male-dominated world. Out of 60 students, only 16 of us were women. Most of the women were steered towards textile design, but that wasn't for me. I wanted to create graphics that made people stop and look, that told a story, that left a mark.

A so-called male friend once told me I'd never make it as a female designer. Well, here's my answer to that; I did make it. I'm still here. And I'm a damn good designer.

In my second year I won the Royal Society of Arts Design Award, a national award that celebrates the very best creative talent. My prize was a trip to New York to visit design studios. Walking into those Manhattan offices was surreal. I thought of that little girl copying Madonna's album cover and realised I'd made it to somewhere that once I only dreamed of.

Seventeen Years in the Game

In my second year of my HND, I got my first job in the design world. My first role was with an American sportswear company, where I designed for huge names like the New York Yankees and Warner Brothers. Then came a job at a publishing company, where I learned the importance of precision and layout design, followed by a role at a packaging company that fuelled my love for seeing a concept come to life on the shelf.

Each of these roles gave me the chance to work with top brands and taught me something new; from understanding how a global brand protects its identity, to the details that make packaging stand out.

Eventually, I moved into agency life, where I stayed for seventeen years. I would like to thank David for my time there. Those years taught me everything: how to manage clients, how to hit impossible deadlines, how to push creative boundaries again and again and, of course, how to play pool and table football (ha ha!).

I worked on incredible accounts including The Barbican, The HAC, Trinity House, Thistle Hotels and Citizen. The work was fast-paced and challenging, but I thrived under pressure and loved seeing ideas turn into finished campaigns.

As studio manager, I was a huge part of running the business making sure that all product designs stayed on brand, invoices were issues and paid promptly, and keeping everything else running smoothly behind the scenes. I also learned how to lay text out the correct way, to absolute perfection, something I still carry into every project I do today.

Those years gave me the confidence to take on anything and the experience to create high-end design work that truly delivers.

The Day Everything Changed

Then suddenly, everything changed. Eleven years ago, I lost my baby son, Harry. There are no words for that kind of pain. It changes you forever. That was the moment I realised life is too short. Too short to stay quiet about what you want. Too short to keep your dreams on the 'one day' shelf. Harry's short life gave me clarity about my own life. It took a while to sink in, but his loss planted a seed that would push me to live bolder, work braver and stop waiting for permission.

Breaking Free

Around this time, I realised that my marriage was falling apart. Nobody walks down the aisle expecting it to end, but over time it became a place where I felt trapped and sad. I found out that my husband had had a girlfriend for over a year before we split up and it not only broke my heart, the kids were devastated too.

There was a lot of love between me and my husband. I wouldn't have married him or had three kids with him if there wasn't. We were together for 23 years and I have fond memories that I cherish to this day. But people change and life changes us. Some of it is for the better, some for the worse. Leaving him wasn't about anger or revenge; it was about my survival and about reclaiming who I was to build a life where my kids could see me happy, thriving, and strong. For over three years I called Women's Aid, knowing I needed to leave him but terrified of what that would mean. Finances are one of the biggest reasons women stay in situations that are breaking them. If you're reading this and you feel trapped, I want you to know there is a way through. Each day, I took one small step forward; one email, one phone call and a quiet plan. The universe has a bigger plan for you, but you must trust it. Starting Claire Louise Branding wasn't just a business decision. It was my lifeline. I promised myself no more. I kept building my business, even on the days I couldn't get out of bed.

Building in the Dark

Life didn't get easier. I became a widow in February 2023.

Suddenly there was no backup plan. No safety net. Just me and three kids without their father, looking to me to hold everything together. And that's the thing about motherhood. You keep going even when every part of you wants to stop. I juggled grief, clients, bills, and managing life one day at a time.

When my dad became unwell last year, I was with him every single day from June until he passed away in October. Between myself and my brother we were looking after Mum, dealing with hospital visits, and keeping daily life ticking over. It was hard.

After Dad passed, my body finally gave in. I developed rheumatoid arthritis, a chronic condition that leaves me with days where the pain is so bad it feels impossible to move.

On top of that, my mum now has vascular dementia and Alzheimer's, and we're supporting her through it every step of the way. I also help care for my mother-in-law, who is disabled. The toll on my health has been enormous, but I keep going. I'm still standing. And I refuse to stop.

Some days I'd sit at my desk with tears rolling down my face, designing through the pain because I had mouths to feed and clients who were counting on me. Those were the days that built my resilience more than anything else.

Life didn't slow down this year either. In July, my eldest daughter Sophie was admitted to hospital while doctors tried to find out what was wrong. At the very same time, my middle daughter Chloe was in the maternity ward having my grandson. For a short while, they were both in the same hospital, one bringing new life into the world, the other facing the scariest health news of her life.

Eventually, Sophie was moved to Queen's Hospital for brain surgery. Just three days after her operation, I was stepping out on the stage at PeakeFest, showing up professionally while still carrying the weight of those hospital corridors with me. Sophie is a fighter. They both are. And they inspire me every single day.

And then there's George, my youngest, who keeps me laughing and reminds me that even on the toughest days, there's still so much joy to be found. His love for football keeps us running from pitch to pitch most weekends. And of course 'COYS'! A little nod to my dad and George's dad, who were both massive Spurs supporters.

The Rise

Claire Louise Branding grew.

I began focusing on work that felt aligned with the level of design I wanted to create. I refined my offers to attract clients who valued the depth and quality of my work, projects that allowed me to bring my full creativity to the table.

I embraced every part of who I am, from my bold ideas to my love of leopard print and the colour red. They became part of my brand, my identity, my unapologetic way of showing up in the world. When I wear red lipstick and leopard print, I feel unstoppable. And that's exactly the energy I bring into every project I touch.

Magic and Intuition

Writing this chapter has been one of the hardest things I've ever done. I cried through most of it. It's raw, it's real, and it took me two weeks past the deadline to finally say, 'I'm done.'

I'm the girl who struggles with writing. Words don't always come easily to me. But design does. Creativity flows through me, and I've learned that my gift isn't just visual.

I'm intuitive. When I work on a brand, I don't just look at colours and fonts. I connect with the business. I feel its energy. I can see what it needs to become.

When I started working on PeakeFest 2025, I remember talking to Nicola and already feeling the event – the venue, the people, even the zebra I saw in my mind as part of the experience. I could feel people taking photos, laughing, connecting, and the energy was electric. Then I went away and brought that vision to life. Walking into the hotel and seeing everything come together – the banners, the table plans, the workbooks, the name cards, even the giant zebra – was a moment I'll never forget. Unlike the big corporate brands where I work with 90-page brand guidelines, this was my chance to be fully free creatively.

Nicola trusted me to let my magic happen and it paid off.

That's the power of letting yourself do what you were born to do.

Creativity isn't just what I do, it's who I am. Music has always been my constant companion. In some ways I'm still that little girl recording the Top 40 on cassette tapes, dreaming of album covers. Now, as a designer, I still have music playing while I work. It feeds my creativity, sets the mood, and helps me tap into the energy of whatever I'm creating.

I also believe in something bigger than me; call it the universe, call it intuition, call it faith. I've learned to trust that bigger plan. Even when things fall apart, even when life takes away what you thought you couldn't live without, the universe is guiding you to where you're meant to be. That belief is what keeps me creating, even on the hardest days.

The Vision Ahead

This isn't the end of my story. It's just the beginning. Everything I've been through has given me scars but those scars are proof I survived. Proof that I got back up, even when life tried to keep me down.

My next chapter is about turning all that experience into something bigger.

I see a future where my work goes beyond design. Where I host webinars to teach business owners how to create brands that truly stand out. Where I run VIP days and masterminds that bring ambitious entrepreneurs both women and men together in powerful spaces. I want to build a community of people who are ready to be bold, to stop hiding, to lead their industries, and to create brands that make them proud.

Everything I've lived through, the loss, the resilience, the rebuilding has made me the person who can lead that space. And I am ready for the next step. If there's one thing, I want you to take from my story, it's this:

Believe in your dreams.

Even when people tell you they're too big.
Even when life knocks you down.
Even when you can't see the next step.

Keep going.

Follow that path, because it does lead to a beautiful destination.
I know, because I'm finding mine right now.

I'm building a business and a life that makes me proud.
I'm raising kids who see that their mum is strong, resilient, and unafraid to create her own future.

And I'm not done yet.

This is just the beginning.

What I've Learned

- Other people's limits don't have to be yours.
- Your portfolio might get you in the door, but your attitude is what keeps you there.
- You don't always get 'someday', so make the most of today.
- Building a business is messy, but it's worth it.
- If you want a premium life, you need to run a premium business.

Acknowledgements

As I finish this chapter, I am filled with gratitude for the people who have walked this journey with me.

To my mum and dad, thank you for believing in me and letting me chase my dreams.

Dad, you were my biggest cheerleader, and I miss you every single day.

To my brother Andy, thank you for encouraging me when I needed it most. Listening to me when I needed it. I just want you to know I love you.

To my three incredible children, Sophie, Chloe, and George you are my 'why', the reason I keep going.

To Harry, my baby boy in heaven you taught me how precious life is. This book is for you too.

To my friends, the list is long. Thank you for standing by me through every storm and every moment of pain. I love you all, especially Maria,

Stacey, Clare and Richard.

To Tony, WOW, what can I say… you are one special human. I'm so excited to see what the future holds.

To my amazing clients, thank you for trusting me with your brands and allowing me to do what I love every single day.

And to Astri, thank you for always believing in me and giving me opportunities to shine.

Life is a rollercoaster. We lose our way; we fall out with the people we love. Some stay, some leave, but love never truly stops.

Dad, I love you with all my heart. This one's for you. Thank you for believing in me, always.

Fiona Forster

Fiona Forster is a qualified Menopause Coach- qualified with certificates and diplomas but more importantly qualified from experience- hers and her clients. She runs face to face sessions on the Southeast Coast and online sessions accessed by women all over the globe. She runs a group coaching programme, her Signature Menopause Plan and also offers 1:1 coaching. She is a member of the British Menopause Society.

https://www.linkedin.com/in/fiona-forster-95777033

Fiona Forster and Embrace the Change

Website: www.embracethechange.org.uk

Insta: Fiona Forster

Feel The Fire But Do It Anyway

Oh, here it comes…that hot, prickly feeling …I feel like I have put my feet on the floor of Death Valley in California. It seems to start at my feet and then, like a rocket, it's at the top of my head. Sometimes, it decides to start at the top and rapidly work its way down. It's like a sudden, volcanic eruption that turns me into a human-sized radiator in approximately 0.3 seconds! I'm burning up and I know my face is as red as a beetroot, beads of sweat are hovering on my top lip, but I carry on the conversation, acting as if nothing is happening…oh how I love hot flushes! Have my listeners even noticed? Some have. My audience begins to wonder if I am ill and whether they should call an ambulance; they are perplexed as to why I am unbuttoning my blouse in public. Well, ladies and gentlemen, if I don't, I will combust and make a terrible mess on the carpet.

Now, as we know, these hot flushes do not only appear during the day; oh no, they appear at night too. As we drift off into a peaceful slumber, we are suddenly soaked in sweat, with sheets like damp ropes twisted around our legs. Hair plastered to our face along with pyjamas stuck to us like glue. Forget the spa ladies - my bed is a sauna! Except the towels are wet and I can't leave politely to get a cold drink. I throw the duvet off and I am cool at last. Bliss! But wait, my furnace has shut down and I'm freezing, shivering and scrambling for the duvet. Does this happen just once? Oh no ladies, it happens 10-12 times some nights! I begin to wonder whether sleep is a myth put forward by the mattress companies.

Don't get me started on make-up. I have given up. You spend ages putting it on, only for it to slide down your face when the hot flush strikes. Mascara? Eyeliner? Err…no! I don't want to look like the Joker when the hot flush strikes.

I think my hypothalamus is on holiday. It should be controlling my temperature – keeping it at a steady 37°C or thereabouts but without my WD40 (oestrogen) and progesterone; and with my hormonal imbalance, well - I can't put all the blame on my hypothalamus. It thinks I am hotter than I am and so widens the blood vessels near to the surface of my skin to cool me down. It also speeds up my heart rate and it activates my sweat glands- what a combination! The room is 21°C but it feels like the Sahara. The hypothalamus calls in the emergency vehicles for a rapid response and opens the flood gates- 'Cool her down.' We are boiling hot then suddenly cool, or cold sometimes to the point of chills (which are multiplying!). So, after blazing like a bonfire, I'm shivering like a penguin on an iceberg! I wonder if we could somehow harness this menopausal heat; it might help with the global energy crisis. These hot flushes have their own timing. I'm giving a work presentation and there it is - flush or a romantic dinner – flush or standing in the supermarket - flush (although this one is probably a well-timed flush as I am sure I can find a freezer somewhere to stick my head in).

As hot flushes are unpredictable and unstoppable, the only real solution is to develop coping strategies. Some women meditate, some fan themselves while looking dignified, and I look like a pigeon frantically flapping my wings to no avail. For me, the most important survival tool for every menopausal woman is a fan (Did I hear you say glass of wine? No!). But I am not talking about a paper fan or a delicate lace fan. No! You need an industrial strength, battery powered device that you can whip out of your handbag at a moment's notice. If you turn it to MAX, the wind will blow your hair and make you look like a film star (well, why not?)

For decades, these hot flushes have been the villain in the story with the whispered 'wait 'til the hot flushes start.' But what would happen if we reframed that? Prepare to come on an adventure with me where we will explore science, silliness and survival tips and when we reach our destination, you might be grateful for nature's gift!

Our hot flushes are a very real, very physical reaction to our shifting hormonal imbalance. It's like gremlins hijacking our temperature gauge. It's uncomfortable, and almost as quickly as it happens it disappears, leaving us cool. This shows our bodies' incredible adaptability.

My body is actually very efficient. It's a menopause calling card: my body's way of saying 'Surprise! We're doing things differently now!'

So grab a tall glass of cool water, put on a loose cotton top, and take a seat ready for departure!

Why would you come with me? Why would you trust me? I am a post-menopausal woman, still getting hot flushes and night sweats from time to time; I am qualified with various menopause certificates and diplomas but far more importantly- I am qualified from experience. Everyone's journey is different so there is no one-size-fits-all solution. One indicator is how your mum or your auntie experienced the menopause. Your experience might be due to hereditary factors but your journey may be different to theirs. However, in general, asking your mum how the menopause was for her is a good indicator for you.

So, bags packed? Passports in hand? Ready for an adventure?

Our first stop on our adventure is a cold, damp February day in the UK. We don't need to worry about being cold as we have our own inbuilt boiler firing on all cylinders. No jumpers needed here. You want to open the window but your partner is shivering. It's possibly blowing a gale outside, but you want to lower your body temperature and as quickly as possible. Your partner wants to steal the duvet- go right ahead. Well, for a little bit anyway. What about walking the dog on a chilly morning…with no coat? We've got this!

Our next stop is the spa or a gym which has a sauna. £30 for half an hour? We don't need that; we have our own inbuilt sauna for free. All this sweating releases the toxins, improves circulation and will leave your skin glowing; once the beetroot flush subsides of course. Sauna? I don't need one; look at the money we are saving!

Let's go spend that money on some clothes but with a twist…We get fashion freedom. We need to wear clothes that let our bodies breathe. Comfort first is the required dress code. Floaty dresses, sleeveless tops, breathable fabrics. No more woollen jackets for us. We have freedom! Layers and more layers are the way to go. Way easier to strip off as the hot flush appears but remember to peel the layers off, we are sophisticated women, so no fumbling around as if we are being attacked by a wasp and his friends.

As we continue our journey, we are joined by many others. We are part of a team; a very special one, and it bonds us. This goes across the generations and unites us. You will recognise a fellow hot flusher and be able to offer support, even if they are a complete stranger. You have found your tribe! It's like a secret handshake; forget networking, forget social media. Have a hot flush in public and you will discover a new sisterhood.

Another money saving hack…. You are more attuned to your body and its changes. You notice that bead of sweat running down your back, your breathing, the feel of your skin and your clothes on said skin. More money saved- no need for expensive mindfulness retreats. We're doing it for ourselves ladies!

What about a visit to an accessories shop? Handheld fan anyone? Neck pillow (could it double up as a travel pillow?). Cooling sprays, cooling sheets for the bed…the list is endless but we have saved money by not going to the sauna or a retreat so we could get lots of accessories.

Next stop Ancient Greece, where older women have the inner fire of the mature woman. Grab your inner fire ladies! They were celebrated and seen as powerful – that's us ladies.

From Greece to the Victorian Era- oh, those bone corsets, those bustles and all those layers- but wait! There are fainting couches or perhaps they should have been called menopause recovery stations?

As we visit the Native Americans, we find 'fire keepers' and, as our tour continues, we find 'konenki' in Japan. It means renewal and energy change. Ladies … this is a new beginning.

We are like the hot flushes. We show up with confidence and no-one is going to stop us. We are unapologetic. Just as they are visible, so are we. Our hot flushes announce that we are very much alive, we've survived decades of life and we are entering this new chapter with heat. There's also a rebellious side to the hot flushes. When women are being told to be 'cool, calm and collected,' they say "No thanks. I'll blaze." Hot flushes are our superpower.

Stop apologising and own The Hot Flush. You are not a sweaty mess, you are a warrior. A warrior – do you want to write that down?

You can stop pretending you are a serene, graceful lady, pretending you are fine with the thermostat set at 'tropical rainforest.' You are on fire, yes literally, but this is your moment, so grab it with both hands.

'Is there a solution?' I hear you scream at the top of your voice. For some, it's HRT. There are two main options; oestrogen only or combined oestrogen and progesterone. There are various ways of getting these hormones into your system; patches, tablets, gels, sprays or the Mirena coil. It depends on where you are on your menopause journey and your particular needs. Going to your GP to discuss your symptoms and which HRT is best for you. There are natural alternatives too. For many, eating a healthier diet, cutting out the alcohol, caffeine, spicy foods, hot drinks and sugar help. This is the time of your life to cherish you and your health. Dress in light layers, use a fan and keep your bedroom cool at night. Exercise is another great solution. I love swimming and am in my own little world as I swim up and down the pool. Maybe your go-to exercise is Zumba, Pilates, Tai Chi or a walk with the dog. Let's get those endorphins going, those happy hormones! Exercise will help with sleep, mood and overall wellbeing too. Give up smoking. Maintain a healthy weight, reduce stress. Yoga, breathing exercises and meditation can help.

I like to think of these hot flushes as power surges. A bit like an electric shock; waking me up and giving me a boost. I am a woman on fire, but oh! What I can achieve! For many of you, the children are older and need you less, so now you have time for you, or you and your partner. What is on your Wishlist? Where do you want to go? What do you want to do? This is a new beginning; it's time for you. What goals would you like to achieve? One of mine was to write a book and here I am. Ok, so it's not a whole book but that's coming!

There are lots of books you can read or listen to. There are podcasts (yup! I've got one of those on the way!). We are so lucky that menopause is not as taboo as it was for our mothers. We can be thankful that people are beginning to understand what is happening to us but remember, they can't understand if you don't tell them! Be open; tell people how you feel and what they can do to help. You are not alone. Hot flushes are not the end of youth, they are the beginning of something better. A stage of life where you can stop caring so much about what others think and start putting yourself and your needs first. Be yourself. Menopause and hot flushes give you permission to stop pretending. We are not 'just going to get on with it' as our mothers and grandmothers did. We are going to thrive! Over half the population are going to go through the menopause and it's a totally natural transition. We are not old, ready to be thrown on the scrap heap. NO! We are now entering a new chapter of our lives; one where we can shine, so let's start this new adventure!

If you've made it this far without spontaneously combusting (or maybe you *have* and you're reading this while draped in a cold towel or sheet), welcome. You've survived the science, the silliness, the sweaty sheets, the supermarket flushes and the spa-that-is-your-body. You're part of the sisterhood now and what a fabulous, feisty bunch we are. Yes! You're part of the tribe now. I am guessing you are either riding the rollercoaster of hot flushes yourself, waiting in the queue to get on the rollercoaster, bracing yourself for the ride or you are supporting someone who is on the rollercoaster.

So, what's next? You are part of our tribe and you do not have to do this alone.

Suffering in silence is so last century. This is the time to speak up, reach out, and get the support you deserve. Whether you're perimenopausal, postmenopausal or somewhere in between with one foot in the fridge and the other in a woolly sock; **help is out there.**

A good place to start is your GP. Go and have a conversation about your symptoms, HRT and whether it's right for you. There are various options and it may take time to find the right HRT for you. Be patient! I realise not all GPs are particularly knowledgeable about the menopause, but some are so see if your surgery has one of those unicorns. Many are catching up. If you don't feel listened to, ask to see a different one, or the menopause nurse if there is one at your surgery. It is important to remember that we are talking about your body, your health, your life. It is also very important to check that your symptoms are indeed menopausal symptoms and not anything else. It's good to get everything checked once in a while!

There may be menopause support groups in your area (NHS or private) where you can meet more of the tribe, women who know exactly what you are going through and who can tell you what worked for them. Swapping survival stories is good for the soul. After all, we survived and have lived to tell the tale. You might find a like-minded community on social media. If your friends are of a similar age to you or older, they may well empathise and have some ideas for you. Sharing is part of the journey and community. Remember it only takes one eye-roll or sweaty brow to recognise a fellow member of our sisterhood.

Podcasts exist (mine is coming!) that discuss 'all things menopause.' Have a listen. Many are by doctors. There are now plenty of books so find one that appeals. Find somewhere cool to sit, with a cool drink and have a read!

Talk to someone. Talk and talk some more. Talk to lots of people. Build your support network around you. Those who won't mind a call at 3.00 am as you lie in bed tangled up with wet sheets, sweating like your life depends on it; someone who will listen and empathise; friends who will come round with cooling sheets and ice cubes (and hot water bottles!). Talk and talk some more. One conversation at a time.

Journalling is a great option. Write about your feelings, what you are grateful for, your stories, your experiences. Put down anything and everything; it is for you and no-one else.

There are natural solutions too. One word of caution: be careful where you get your information from and do a little digging. We do not need special face creams described as 'menopausal skin creams' and, likewise with supplements, choose carefully. The NHS has lots of resources available.

Nutritionists, personal trainers, coaches - there are a lot of people on your side, ready to listen and offer support.

Whether you are in the boardroom, on fire (literally!) or walking up and down the frozen food aisle, opening door after door (well, as many as is deemed acceptable in one visit) you deserve to feel supported, understood and empowered.

This is not the end; this is the start of something fierce. We are not fading. We are on fire, like our hot flushes. We are unapologetic and flaming.

And finally, don't forget the fun.

Yes, it's sweaty. Yes, it's wild. Yes, it's a hormonal rollercoaster, a hayride. But it's also a sign that we've lived, we've learned, and now we get to **lead.** We are not fading away. We are not invisible. We are showing up shiny, glowy, a little damp and we are absolutely unstoppable.

So, tell your story. Ask the questions. Own the flushes. And if anyone says you're 'too hot to handle' just smile, whip out your industrial-strength fan, and say, 'Damn right I am.'

Jo Shelton

I'm Jo Shelton, founder of the She Takes Action Network, a global movement helping women (especially 50+) turn travel into transformation and build freedom-led businesses online.

After 35+ years in business, I've survived burnout, rebuilt after rock bottom, and now lead with heart, hustle, and a whole lot of bold. From losing 13 stone and reclaiming my health, to launching a brand that empowers women to stop playing small, I'm living proof it's never too late.

Ready to shake the system and show what's possible? Let's get unapologetically loud, visible, and free.

https://linkmate.one/Jo_Shelton

The Rebirth of a Woman Who Refused to Stay Invisible

I wasn't supposed to be here. Not on this page. Not living life on my terms. Not building a global movement in my fifties. Not standing on stages, launching podcasts, mentoring women, or running a business from my phone. I was supposed to fade quietly. Shrink. Disappear.

But let me tell you something...

I am not the woman you bury quietly. I am the woman who BURNS THE BOX she was put in.

My name is Jo Shelton. I'm 57 years old, a Nana of three, and I've been in the game, the real game of business, leadership, and survival for over 35 years.

I've sold the lotions. I've hosted the parties. I've hustled until my soul was burnt out and my body was broken. I've cried on the bathroom floor. I've reset to zero more times than I care to admit. I've watched people rise through ranks by faking it, fluffing it, and burning out women like me who gave everything, and still felt like it wasn't enough.

Then one day... I looked in the mirror, all 29 stone of me and said: "Jo, this can't be it. There has to be more than this."

That was the start of my boldest chapter.

So, who am I?

I'm not your typical 57-year-old. I'm young at heart but wise from the wounds. I've built multiple businesses, mentored thousands, and walked away from anything that no longer aligned with the woman I was becoming. I had gastric sleeve surgery in 2023 and lost 13 stone; not just physically, but emotionally too. I didn't just shed weight; I shed shame. I shed stories that weren't mine and I rebuilt myself from scratch, body, brand, and belief system.

I'm now the CEO of the She Takes Action Network (STAN), a movement of ambitious, purpose-driven women who are DONE waiting to be chosen. We travel the world. We earn income online. We build empires, not excuses and we do it all with heart, hustle, and zero apology.

So, what's this chapter about?

This chapter is not about the highlights reel. This is about the invisible years. The moments I almost gave up. The seasons where I shrank my dreams to fit other people's comfort zones and the radical decision to stop surviving and start showing up BOLD AS F*CK.

You're going to read about the truth of starting over after 50. What it means to lead a movement when the world tells you to sit down and be quiet. What it takes to get visible when you feel invisible and how building a freedom business that isn't just a goal, it's a rebellion.

Why am I writing this?

I am writing this chapter because I know there's a woman reading this who feels like she missed her chance. She's scrolling, watching, cheering for others, but deep down, wondering if there's more for her too.

Let me make this clear…

This is your f*cking sign.

You don't need a perfect body, perfect plan or perfect past. You just need to get loud about what you want and dangerous about not settling anymore.

I'm going to walk you through how I went from being forgotten to financially free. From burnout to building a brand that makes me wake up excited again and how YOU can take the mic back in your own life and start leading, earning, and living like the bold woman you were born to be.

So, buckle up because I'm not here to make you feel good.

I'm here to wake-you-the-hell up.

Let's go.

SECTION ONE: The Breaking Point

'You're in a Lot of Pain, Aren't You?'

Did you ever have one of those moments where someone sees you, really sees you, and all the walls you've been holding up just crumbled?

That moment came for me after three years of being ignored. Three years of being gaslit by the very people who were supposed to help. Three years of being in pain so deep, I had to crawl up the stairs like a child…or sleep on the sofa next to a commode just to survive.

I didn't 'choose' gastric sleeve surgery as some shiny self-help decision. I didn't wake up inspired and start a transformation journey with a planner and a Pinterest quote.

I woke up in unbearable pain. Couldn't walk. Couldn't stand and when I went to the doctor?

Dismissed. Eye rolls. 'Lose some weight and move more'

Move more? I couldn't even get to the toilet.

They didn't listen. They didn't test. Just pushed painkillers across the desk and sent me on my way.

They scanned my hands when the problem was in my knees. They called it weight-related pain when it was actually aggressive, undiagnosed arthritis.

Years of misdiagnosis. Years of silent suffering.

Until one day, I met an American locum doctor. She looked at me, paused, and said, 'You're in a lot of pain, aren't you?'

I broke. I sobbed from relief.

She sent me for the tests I had begged for. MRI. X-rays. The truth finally came out; torn cartilage in both knees. Rheumatoid arthritis. Osteoarthritis. Degeneration and a family history of it which was there in my records.

All ignored because I was overweight, I was a woman and because I was easy to dismiss.

But that one doctor saw me and because I had been left untreated for so long, they threw everything at me: pain clinics, weight management, and eventually... the offer of gastric sleeve surgery on the NHS.

I said yes. Not because I was weak but because I wanted my damn life back.

That moment cracked something open in me. The old Jo, the silenced, people-pleasing, invisible Jo, started to die.

Pain didn't just break me. It birthed me.

SECTION TWO: Rebuilding From the Rubble

From Pain to Power: The War I Didn't Choose, and the Freedom I Fought For.

Do you know what no one tells you? That sometimes your rebirth starts in a wheelchair.

Mine did.

The damage to my knees was irreversible. I couldn't walk unaided. My independence was stolen. My self-worth shattered and the weight I carried was more than physical. It was decades of shame, silence and swallowed pain.

Social services delivered a commode. I couldn't climb stairs. I crawled.

I was suicidal. Alone and I didn't know how much longer I could take it.

However, this industry, this profession of network marketing, coaching, leading women, it saved me.

Even when I was stuck on a sofa, I still had my phone. I still had a mission. I still had the spark of a voice that refused to be silenced. So, when the NHS offered me gastric sleeve surgery, I took it. It was never about vanity. It was about freedom.

I lost over 13 stone. But I gained back everything else.

My dignity. My power. My voice and I used that voice to build the She Takes Action Network, a space for women (especially the over 50s) who are DONE being invisible. We travel. We earn. We rise. We go live scared. We speak up even when our voice shakes. We press 'post' even when we think no one is watching. We do it together and every time one woman gets louder, the rest of us get braver.

I know how it feels to be alone and because of that I will spend the rest of my life making sure no woman ever feels that again.

I still live with pain. I'm now awaiting a double knee replacement, but pain doesn't own me anymore. I decided to rise anyway because I chose bold and because I said: ENOUGH.

SECTION THREE: The Unapologetic Rise

Visibility is My Rebellion.

The moment I started showing up online, visibly, vocally, and unapologetically, everything changed.

I wasn't waiting to be picked anymore. I wasn't asking if it was okay to speak. I stopped toning myself down to make other people comfortable and guess what? The right women started listening. The ones who felt what I had been through. The ones who had shrunk themselves for decades. The ones who were ready to rise but just needed someone to show them how.

When I started doing Facebook Lives from my sofa, pain in my knees, fear in my throat, I realised something:

You don't need to be perfect to be powerful.

You just need to go first.

So, I did and what I found was more than an audience. I found a movement.

STAN wasn't just a business idea; it was my battle cry. For every woman (especially over 50s) who's been told her best years are behind her. For every Nana who's been told to slow down. For every leader who's never been given the mic.

I claimed the mic and now I pass it to others.

We rise together. We build together. We travel together. We take action, bold, messy, 'visible AF' action, and we never apologise for who we are.

We are legacy leaders. Not just building income, but impact. Not just showing up but showing the f*ck up.

We are rewriting the rules for women (especially the over 50s) who were told their time had passed. We say: the best years are the ones we're about to create.

This year, I stood on stage for the very first time, just a few minutes, introducing myself and sharing a glimpse of my story as part of this powerful collaboration. I was scared as hell, but nothing changes if nothing changes. I've built income from my sofa, with swollen knees and a tray table, showing up messy but committed. I've helped other women go from burnt out to building businesses that light them the f*ck up and I'm just getting started.

So, if you're reading this wondering if there's more for you? If you're scrolling, watching, liking everyone else's highlight reel but thinking… 'Why not me?'

This is your wake-up call.

Don't wait to feel ready. Don't wait to lose the weight, fix the past, or get the permission slip.

Take the damn mic.

Be bold. Be loud. Be visible and build the life you were born for, not the one you were handed.

CALL TO ACTION:

- Follow me on Instagram: @JoSheltonOfficial
- Facebook: @JoSheltonOfficial
- Join the movement: Facebook Group: She Takes Action Network: Empowering Women Through Travel & Business (Website Coming Soon.)

- DM me 'BOLD AS F*CK' if you're ready to stop watching and start leading.

Let's f*cking go.

Jo Shelton

FROM PAGE TO ACTION: Your Next Move

Reading this chapter might have stirred something deep in your gut, a flicker of 'maybe I can' or a full-blown fire of 'I'm ready to rise.' Either way, don't let it fizzle out. Let it move you.

I've been where you are and I have built the She Takes Action Network™ for women like us, bold, bruised, brilliant, and DONE playing small.
So where do you start?

- Start by deciding. Decide you're done being invisible. Decide you're worthy. That's step one, a choice, not a condition.
- Take up space. Post something real today. Message someone bold. Share your story. You don't need a big audience. You just need to begin.
- Plug into a circle that sees you. Come find us inside STAN. We're your people, ambitious, messy, unstoppable.
- Ditch perfection. Progress beats perfection. Start before you're ready. Ready is a myth.

If you're scared, GOOD. It means this matters.

DM me 'NEXT MOVE' and I'll help you take your first bold step because it's never too late to rewrite your story and yours is just beginning.

A TRIBUTE TO THE WOMAN WHO SHOWED ME WHAT'S POSSIBLE

Before I ever stood on a stage, before I ever believed my story mattered, there was one woman I followed who changed everything for me:

Jessie Lee Ward.

She didn't just teach business. She embodied unapologetic leadership. She showed up bold, brilliant, and unfiltered; and in doing so, gave women like me permission to do the same.
When I was in pain, she spoke life. When I was invisible, she showed me how to become undeniable.

She left a legacy, not just in earnings, but in impact and part of that lives through this chapter, through me, and through every woman I now serve.

Thank you, Jessie Lee. You'll never be forgotten.

We keep going. We keep building. We stay bold.

#LongLiveJLW.

Mike Calder

A safari guide since 2014, his wildlife passion began thirty years before that. A keen photographer, his wildlife imagery has hung on gallery walls worldwide and featured in conservation campaigns.

He draws lessons from wildlife to inspire resilience, leadership and legacy. Through retreats, writing and visual storytelling he invites readers to rediscover their connection to nature and themselves, to inspire personal growth and purposeful leadership.

Mike's work reminds us that the wild lives within us, guiding how we live, lead and leave our mark on the world. A bridge between the wild and the human spirit.

I invite you to connect with me on LinkedIn (and other platforms) by scanning this QR code:

Wild Purpose

We stopped to look back across the valley. The elephant was still following and gaining ground. He did have, after all, some extra leg power! Four versus our two.

I had recently qualified as a safari guide and was now undertaking specialist training in delivering walking safaris in areas with dangerous animals. The so-called Big Five.

For eight weeks I walked and walked. No longer feeling protected by the steel plates of a game-viewing vehicle. A backpack filled with five litres of water, a modest lunch of fruit and clingfilm-wrapped sandwiches, burning calories with every step over hills, through tall grasses, always under the continuous South African summer sun. I had drunk all the water by the end of each day.

I listened as my guide trainer, Pieter, offered his thoughts on why the elephant was following us. Maybe he feels threatened, or perhaps curious about the new scents left along the route we had walked. Who was trespassing in *his house*? The hot sunshine and our evaporating sweat went hand in hand, as did the traces of Dove, Nivea or Sure deodorant that we used to mask our natural body odours. Not masked for the benefit of the animals, but from one another.

An elephant's sense of smell is extraordinary, being twice as strong as the dog stopping frequently on their daily walk. Up to two thousand olfactory receptor genes allow an elephant to detect water twelve miles away.

We were much closer than that, perhaps only a thousand metres away, but standing on elevated ground. Through binoculars we could see the elephant sniffing the ground with his trunk. I imagined the scents bombarding him: the floral notes, sandalwood, vanilla, apple and citrus. And unmistakably the smell of a human! All those scent molecules sparking synapses in the elephant's brain.

Was it similar to how we feel catching the aroma of coffee or baked bread? Scent marketing is everywhere in our daily lives. Vanilla and coffee encourage us to change our behaviour, and woody aromas drifting through a bookstore encourage us to linger.

I loved walking and learning about the wildlife around me. In a vehicle, you might speed past a flowering tree and catch only a fleeting waft, but on foot the scents linger. You can sense the animals nearby, hear birdsong more clearly without the wind rushing past our ears and observe subtle behaviours as they unfold. You live it, in every sense of the word.

Feel it.

Hear it.

See it.

Smell it.

And even taste it!

I hadn't always been a safari guide but my family's connection to Africa stretched back to the 1960's, when my dad had worked first in Uganda and later in Ghana. I grew up leafing through family photo albums filled with grainy, colour or black and white images of zebras, giraffes, elephants, and my family.

In 1988 Sigourney Weaver starred in the Hollywood adaptation of Dian Fossey's memoir of her years studying the mountain gorillas in Rwanda, *Gorillas In The Mist*.

The movie did a remarkable job of showing the challenges of conservation. Habitat loss, cultural sensitivities, communicable diseases, conflict between humans and wildlife over the same resources and, heartbreakingly, poaching.

It was a movie that left a lasting impression on me. At twelve years old, I already had a strong sense of justice, and the idea of poaching horrified me, especially the thought of gorilla hands being turned into ashtrays to be sold as souvenirs!

What the actual fuck was wrong with people?

Over the next few years, I kept being moved by conservation themes. The campaigns like Save the Whales, the Dolphins or the Tigers. At school I threw myself into the sciences. Biology and chemistry were my favourite subjects. What is life? And how does life work, from a single cell to a complex lifeform?

At school, teachers suggested that working with animals might suit me. It didn't work out that way back then. Like many, my first job was in hospitality working in fast food. I was quickly promoted to assistant manager and from there to a role as a chef. A job that relied on two senses important to me: taste and smell.

In 2001 I was invited to visit my dad, who was then working in South Africa. He promised to take me on a safari if I took time off work. I said yes! I still have the photographs from that trip, my first real pictures of wild animals. Luckily, at dusk we encountered a leopard that posed just a few feet away from the vehicle. Then it yawned- click- what a set of teeth! Their canine teeth are the longest of any big cat in proportion to body size. The leopard climbed a nearby tree and posed again, gazing into the distance, silhouetted in the fading light. Click.

The next morning brought another stroke of luck: a pair of cheetahs climbed onto a fallen tree, about shoulder height and used the bark as a scratching post. We were so close I felt I could almost reach out and touch one. I remember the raking sound of claws being sharpened against bark, being readied to hook into a fleeing gazelle at forty miles an hour.

That same afternoon, we came upon a lion pride with five cubs. The adults lay sprawled on the ground while the restless cubs played, clambering over them. It was like watching a David Attenborough wildlife documentary unfold before my eyes. The scene was complete, with the dry, dusty smell of the bush.

The next day one of the guides offered to take me out into the bush on foot. The guide carried only a walkie-talkie and a rifle. I asked him, 'Will you have time to aim and shoot if we are attacked?' His reply was simple. 'No'. Many years later, during my own guide training, I learned why. A leopard can cover twenty-four metres in a single second, smashing Usain Bolt's 100 metre world record by five seconds. Even a hippopotamus, often thought of as lumbering, can run at eleven metres per second- fast enough to outpace the fastest human. And that is the *slowest* of the large mammals and big cats. The guide added, 'If we encounter anything, follow my instructions and don't run!'

And with that we set off. I felt exposed, vulnerable, keenly aware that lions, buffalo, leopards and elephants were somewhere out there. Adrenaline surged around my body. I remember little of that walk, beyond following closely behind my guide. Years of long hours working in kitchens and a non-existent exercise routine, had left me unprepared to regulate that adrenaline. The guide spoke only occasionally, and that silence was my fault. I was overwhelmed, my natural curiosity muted, and questions left unasked. Hyper-vigilance consumed me. The walk ended without incident- and yet I felt alive for having done it!

I went back to the UK and continued my career as a chef working in London, the Cotswolds and the South West. I even won an award. And I still wasn't fulfilled. In 2009 I was left some money after my stepmum died from cancer. The 2008 credit crunch had left the job market stagnant, so I searched the internet for something that might ignite a fire inside me.

I found two things that stood out.

- I could go to South Africa and train to be a safari guide! But I didn't have enough funds.

- I could qualify as an English Teacher and teach English abroad as a foreign language, in China.

Before making the only choice, I used some of the funds for a quick trip to Namibia, to meet friends I'd made working in hospitality. I was back in Africa, this time, a new country to explore. Etosha National Park, once the largest protected reserve on earth, awaited me. A protected area home to black rhino, elephant and the big cats. It was my first time abroad since the safari with my dad in South Africa. Namibia is a land of contrasts, with towering sand dunes in the oldest desert, Africa's largest canyon, second in the world to the Grand Canyon in the US, to the blinding brilliance of Etosha's white clay salt pan, visible from space. I loved every minute of it!

Back in the UK, after months of study, I completed teacher training, working on assignments after grueling shifts spent in the kitchen. As an uncle to eight and godfather to two, I've often been told that I have a way with kids. I'd also enjoyed training young people during my decade working in hospitality and it was life coaching for some of them. I saw teaching as upskilling.

Most of the hospitality roles I'd had were behind the scenes, but now I would be standing in front of classrooms of thirty or more children. As we age, we start to censor what we say to protect others from embarrassment or shield ourselves from judgement. Teenagers know this instinctively. Many of my teenage students were silent in class, reluctant to make a mistake in a foreign language in front of peers. The younger students were uninhibited and enjoyed the activities of my lessons. Often their parents watched silently, from the back of the class.

I had never been further from my comfort zone.

I was offered a new year-long contract. Proof that I had done well, but I declined the opportunity. The teaching position was located in Inner Mongolia, an autonomous region in China. I spent the winter there. It was cold. Bitterly cold. Close to the Gobi Desert, the dry frigid air didn't even ice up the car windscreens, although daily temperatures dropped to -20°C. Language was another barrier. Few spoke English outside of the school and my attempts at Mandarin went misunderstood. It was early 2011, before Google Maps or Google Translate were fully launched in China. There was little comfort in that zone, and I returned to hospitality in the UK. But I knew that I had taken a Bold as Fuck step.

Back in the UK, I watched a television documentary called *Survival With Ray Mears*, where he tracked some of the world's deadliest predators: wolves, bears & leopards. The episode on leopards fascinated me the most. I recognised the location, a reserve in Namibia I had visited with my friends. And even some of the same staff appeared on screen. Ray Mears is a bushcraft master whose shows I had followed for years. Now three of my interests had aligned: Namibia, leopards and Ray. When I checked his website out and saw he was planning an expedition to Namibia the following year to continue to track the featured leopards, I was instantly hooked. I was in! Sold! Back in 1963 Dian Fossey had taken out an $8000 loan to fund her journey to Africa and her conservation of mountain gorillas. In the same spirit, I borrowed money to fund my own trip.

So, in 2012 I spent 10 nights with Ray Mears on his expedition. We were assigned two safari guides and trackers from the Khoisan people, an indigenous group of hunter-gatherers in southern Africa. Renowned for their persistence, the Khoisan are legendary trackers able to follow the faintest trail over many miles. Traditionally they hunt with arrows, the tips dipped in poison derived from plants and the larvae of beetles. Depending on the dosage and the size of the animal, death could take only hours or even days. And there is no general antidote, as the toxins from the plants or larvae work in different ways. Watching their skill was humbling. They read the ground for tracks while running, as easily as we might notice tyre marks in mud. Their persistence was survival in action. Purpose as clear as any lion hunting an antelope, to feed themselves and their offspring.

I also noticed the workday routines of our guides: the tasks of equipping the vehicles with refreshments, blankets and first aid kits. I noticed their passion when they spoke about the animals we encountered. It is a privilege to be able to witness nature unfold before you. The tense standoff between predator and prey: the steely gaze of a lioness fixed on an antelope and the snort of alarm in reply, to alert their herd. Over those ten days I became certain that this was something I wanted to do. I admired the reserve's conservation management team of ecologists and its anti-poaching unit working to protect the wildlife, endangered or not. Because when you protect one keystone species like rhino, you create a broader safety net that shelters everything in the ecosystem.

I returned multiple times to this reserve, just as countless documentary production crews did over the following years, filming content for the BBC's flagship shows helmed by *Deadly 60's* Steve Baskshall or narrated by Sir David Attenborough. I never saw the leopard from Ray Mears' documentary episode, but we did find its pawprints in the sand as the leopard had a distinctly shaped toe on one paw. Learning to read the signs left in sand & mud, or the disrupted foliage, is a skill that we have lost in our concrete jungles. Drag marks could signify a struggle between predator or prey. Our guides described it as 'reading the bush newspaper' each morning. Like detectives piecing together the events of a nightclub brawl, safari guides will read the tracks left behind at a water hole during the night. A story of success, failure or survival, the circle of life, in paw prints and hooves.

I knew that safari had me hooked and I needed to get qualified. The solution to my financial hurdle came the following year, though at a heavy price. Cancer, which had already taken my stepmum, struck again, this time claiming my dad. Another pillar of my support system was gone. But his inheritance gave me the funds to pursue the career I had always longed for.

After months of online research, I chose an accredited guide training school and in June 2014 I arrived in Port Elizabeth (renamed in 2021 to Ggebehra) eager to learn in the Eastern Cape of South Africa. My fellow students, ranging in age from eighteen to forty-eight, came from across the world. Together we absorbed the knowledge both from the textbooks and the outdoor classroom itself. Training seemed to flash by, and exam week arrived. I wasn't ready. The natural year is a rhythm of seasons and rainfall: grasses sprouting, flowers blooming, antelope giving birth, predators rearing hungry cubs, the dry season tightening its grip. The circle of life in cycles I hadn't yet learned to read deeply enough.

So, I failed myself and repeated the training. To onlookers it might have looked like self-sabotage, but for me it was about building the confidence to truly call myself a safari guide. I needed to know more. Repeating modules cemented what I had learned and expanded my knowledge base. Exam time came around again, bringing both a written exam and a three hour long practical assessment, driving guests on a real game drive, complete with a refreshment stop. I scored 99% on the written exam. The practical made me nervous. At first, there were no antelope, giraffe, zebra or elephant in sight. But safari guide training prepares you for that. It wasn't long until I found my rhythm: I pointed out birds, then plants and trees, historically used in treating headaches or even brushing teeth. And finally, we encountered some larger animals to observe, which is the main reason many will go on a safari. I had some happy guests to entertain on the refreshment break. I passed and graduated onto the specialist courses. Advanced Rifle Handling and Walking Safaris.

I tried to find work in South Africa or Namibia, but government policy rightly prioritised hiring local citizens. I thought that my skillsets: being an English teacher, chef and qualified safari guide would make me an asset for the reserves, for both clients and the community. The career door closed.

Bouncing back, I set up my own company in 2016. I donated images for Varta Batteries to be used in their anti-poaching campaigns, and I arranged safaris. Nothing, however, prepared me for the upheaval of 2020 as borders closed and the travel industry collapsed. Bookings were cancelled, jobs on reserves in South Africa and Namibia were lost. The funding of anti-poaching units faltered, and the poachers grew bolder.

I had to close my company, and my 32-year-old dream was suddenly over. The inheritance from my dad was gone and I couldn't see how to revive what I'd worked so long for. I sank into depression for the next two years. I went back to the kitchen once more. As lockdowns eased and social distancing measures lifted, I began to work six or seven days a week. In 2022, after two years grounded by Covid and financial strain, I returned to Namibia. Reconnecting with old friends was a joy, but it was the wildlife that truly healed me. Being among them was medicine for my soul. By 2023 I could see a way forward and the following year I realised the deeper truth, the importance of having a purpose. My purpose has given me resilience. Nature heals and conserving nature heals our planet. A healing cycle.

Now as I write these words in late 2025, I know that I wouldn't still be on this entrepreneurial journey without that strong sense of purpose. To persist when doors slam shut, to endure when the world throws up a shitstorm, to choose wisely where to invest in spreading awareness of the natural world.

Being in the wild and connecting with nature helped me navigate grief. From wildlife, we can observe persistence, resilience and purpose.

These are all needed in our lives, but in our entrepreneurial endeavors, purpose is the keystone.

And when you stay true to yourself, opportunities can arrive. I am now a globally exhibited wildlife photographer, with work featured on walls, in magazines and in community campaigns, raising awareness of poaching around Namibia.

I never thought I'd say that.

Be bold.

Be Bold as Fuck

Magic lives on the other side.

******

Connect with me on LinkedIn for my newsletter *Wild Purpose* and let me take you into nature.

Nicola Peake

Nicola Peake is the founder of Peake Event Group and creator of PeakeFest - the boldest business festival in the UK. Known for her unapologetic honesty and fearless energy, she helps entrepreneurs create, fill, and monetise events that make an impact. From small retreats to large-scale festivals, Nicola has built a reputation for doing things differently - with heart, humour, and a healthy dose of boldness. After being knocked down more than once, she's proof that, courage, and connection can rebuild anything. Her mission? To help others be seen, heard, and boldly unstoppable.

https://www.facebook.com/nicola.peake.9

https://www.instagram.com/nicola.peake_peake.event.group

https://www.PeakeFest.co.uk/

https://www.linkedin.com/in/nicola-peake

The 'Bold as Fuck' Come Back.

Being 'Bold as Fuck' isn't something I would have ever called myself a few years ago, but looking back, I always was. Whenever someone would tell me how brave I was, how much I inspired them, I would play it down, laugh it off with things like, 'I'm just a bit nuts," or 'I get bored easily.' Deep down, I've always carried this belief that I'm just… average.

I never thought of it as a negative thing. It was simply the story I had told myself for years. But the people who've championed me, supported me, and witnessed the things I've actually done were the ones who challenged that belief. They would remind me that no one 'average' would ever take on the challenges I've faced or turn wild visions into reality the way I have.

And now, at the ripe age of 46, I'm finally realising the truth, that those beliefs were complete bullshit. The reality?

I am, and always have been, 'Bold as Fuck'.

What beliefs are you carrying that are holding you back? What do you play down or laugh off? Deep down, do you already know you've done things that are bold as fuck, but you won't own them. I want you to start rewriting those beliefs the way I have. I want you to see how fucking amazing you really are. Because when that switch flicks the right way no one can stand in your way.

I learned this the hard way. Last year I let a handful of people's words and actions completely strip me of my power. And when I look back, I'm more annoyed with myself than with them. After everything I've done in this life how the hell did I let peoples judgement make me hide, shrink, doubt myself, and believe I fucked up and going forward I should just stay average?

For months that is exactly what I did.

Average feels safe. Average doesn't get you called out online. Average doesn't grab attention. Average doesn't make people want to tear you down. And I think that's why I carried it. It felt easier. But the truth is, it started way before that.

It started with little Nicola. Loud Nicola. Nicola who said the wrong thing at the wrong time. Nicola who made big decisions and took risks in her twenties that didn't always pay off. Nicola who became a financial adviser at 23 in a male-dominated world and was told she was the most unprofessional person they knew because she did her nails in her lunch break. Nicola who topped the league tables again and again but had the glory taken away by male managers who dismissed her and introduced her as 'the single mum.'

Nicola who was told by an older woman that she looked amazing…. until she opened her mouth. Nicola who was made to sit at the front of the class by her nun teacher because she was 'a bastard.' Nicola whose dad never bothered with her. Nicola who was mentally and physically abused by a man. Nicola who has always felt disliked.

All of these things could fill a series of books, but they left me carrying beliefs for years. That I didn't matter much. That I wasn't special. That I didn't fit in. That I was just average.

I guess that's one of the reasons I've always strived to do bigger things, to prove people wrong. And last year, after taking on the biggest challenge of my life, I felt so fucking proud. I felt like the most 'average' woman had just done something completely not average, and I was buzzing. I was on top of the world.

Until I wasn't.

That safety I had always hidden behind, the thing I finally stepped out from, came crashing down. Everything I ever feared happened. And do you know what I did? I went straight back into my shell. Playing small, hiding, and making myself extremely average again.

I stopped showing up, stopped selling and stopped attending events. And in that space, I let my beliefs, along with a handful of people's actions, drag me right back. It was like every painful moment I had ever carried rolled into one mammoth ball of hurt. All of it crashing into me at once.

This is exactly why I'm writing about being bold. I'm not going to sit here and tell you to just 'show up, be brave, be bold' like it's some quick fix. Because it isn't. It's not easy. It's not something you can flick on overnight.

But if my story helps you in any way, if it reminds you to never hand your power over, if it gives you the strength to stop letting anyone make you small or hold you back from what you love, then I've done what I came here to do. That, to me, is success. Because it means I've gone beyond average once again.

Stop waiting.

Stop playing small.

I bet you've already done things that prove how bold you are, even if you've brushed them off or buried them under old beliefs. Own them, celebrate them and build from them.

Because once you decide you're bold as fuck, everything shifts. You stop apologising. You stop second-guessing, and you stop giving your power away. When that happens, no one can tear you down, because you finally know exactly who the hell you are.

What's your story? What beliefs are you holding onto that do you no justice at all? How long are you going to let them run the show?

Take a minute and write this down:

- What is the belief I've been carrying about myself that isn't true?
- Where did it come from?
- What is the truth I want to replace it with?
- If I owned how bold I really am, what would change for me?

Because the world doesn't need you smaller, safer, or quieter. It needs you bolder. This is where my story takes a turn. Because while I was wrestling with these beliefs about being average, I went and did the most un-average thing of my entire life. I had this wild idea, to hold a business conference in a field. Not in a hotel ballroom, not in a conference centre, but in a bloody field. Who does that? Me, apparently. A woman who had never done anything like it before decided to take on a challenge that most people wouldn't even dream of.

For a year I worked on making it happen. I faced challenge after challenge with venues, suppliers, logistics, you name it. And still, I built a huge community around the vision. Over 1,000 people showed up online for the launch. They loved the concept, the energy, the newness of it. I made myself visible in ways I never had before. I sponsored events. I promoted it non-stop. And the results came; over 400 tickets sold and six figures in sponsorship raised.

This event was a vision I brought to life. I watched it get built in front of my eyes, the stage, the big top, the bar, the posh loos, the festoon lights, the flags, the tipis, even the bloody bins and water pipes. All the behind-the-scenes nightmares no one else sees. But I saw them. I dealt with them. I created a £250k turnover festival from scratch with zero experience.

This was not average. This was not safe. This was not playing small.

The vision that had lived in my head for over a year was suddenly standing in front of me, alive and real.

I remember walking through the site in the final hours before it opened and just stopping to take it all in. The stage was up, bold and beautiful. The flags were flying. The lights were strung across the field, waiting to glow as the sun went down. The big top stood tall, a mix of magic and madness that I had somehow pulled off. People were arriving, pitching tents, grabbing drinks, and for the first time I thought, 'I actually did it.'

I felt proud in a way that I had never felt proud before. Not just because of the logistics, the sponsors, or the money raised, but because I had turned an idea that lived in my head into a living, breathing reality. I had created a space for people to connect, to do business differently, to laugh, to share stories, to dance under the lights.

In that moment, standing in a field surrounded by everything I had built, I didn't feel average at all.

I felt extraordinary.

I felt bold as fuck.

It was a high like no other. The energy, the love, the buzz. People were telling me how incredible it was, how it felt different to anything they had ever been to before. I saw friendships forming, deals being made, people stepping up on stage and being seen in a whole new way. For once, I let myself breathe it in. For once, I let myself believe it. An average person doing non average things.

Then came the hard bit. Not the smiling photos or the highlight reels people shared afterwards. The real behind-the-scenes stuff no one ever sees.

I was exhausted. I had never done anything on this scale before, and it showed. Delegating wasn't easy because we were all learning. None of us had run a festival before, so everyone was figuring it out as we went along, and of course looking to me for the answers. The truth was, I didn't really know. I hadn't been fully prepared for just how much work it would take. That was on me.

We had days of torrential rain before the event, then cold and windy weather all weekend. Half the people who had tickets couldn't get there. The ground was wet and with it came problem after problem. I wasn't the one physically pulling cars out, but I was the one everyone came to when something went wrong. 'Nic, what do we do about this?' 'Nic, we've got a problem here.' 'Nic, can you find someone?'

When you're responsible for the safety of hundreds of people, the pressure is huge. I was keeping an eye on wind speeds, checking structures were safe, watching build teams adapt last-minute because of the weather. Attendees don't see any of that, but those decisions mattered more than whether I had time to walk around chatting or sit down for five minutes.

I put my heart and soul into it. The feedback afterwards was unreal. Socials blew up with posts, reviews, stories. Most people bloody loved it. But of course, not everyone did. My daughters overheard gossip in the food queues. I caught sharp comments in passing. And when you're a people pleaser who wants everyone to have the best time, it hurts when you feel like you've let people down.

But what came next was worse. Because the noise didn't stop when the festival ended. Two weeks later, it moved online.

I spent two weeks recovering, sleeping, resting and enjoying all the positive feedback. I had sold around 70 tickets to the next PeakeFest, and I was getting back to business.

Of course, there were difficult conversations to have, and yes, I received some negative messages and comments. Did I handle them all with a level head? No. When something feels personal and the criticism comes sharp instead of constructive, it's not easy to take.

But looking back, I see it for what it was, a symptom of me doing something bigger. I had put myself out there, taken risks. And with that comes challenges.

Then the online downpour hit. Two weeks after the festival the posts started, and the criticism quickly turned from the event to me. I woke up one Saturday morning feeling broken, lying in bed in tears, with negative post after negative post appearing. Every mistake was being called out, even the bloody weather. It went absolutely mad. People fuelled the threads and it carried on for days. I never once read the comments underneath. I knew the gist and I didn't need to make myself feel worse. I deleted Facebook and stayed off it for about two weeks.

The fallout carried on long after. I lost clients. People who had supported me at the start, who had posted about what an amazing time they had, stopped engaging with me and quietly left my spaces. Others unfriended me. People I had been close to stopped liking or commenting because they didn't want to be seen with me. It was one of the worst times of my life. People see posts and wade in, not thinking about the impact it has on someone long term.

For months after, almost every week, I would hear about conversations where my name came up. People who had never met me saying PeakeFest was a failure. I even heard voice notes of people saying they wanted nothing to do with me, that I wasn't welcome at their events, that they didn't want their reputation ruined by being associated with me.

That's when I gave up my power. I started to believe the noise. I felt like I had to apologise for my own event. I stopped talking about it. I stopped sharing it. I played it down. Week by week I retreated from my business, from people, and from myself. I got so nervous about seeing anyone, that I couldn't even face small mastermind days. I would shake like a leaf, just like I did in school when I was forced to speak up in class. I didn't know who I could trust, who secretly hated me, and who didn't. It messed with my head completely. I got quieter, moodier, unhappy, numb, and depressed.

I debated cancelling PeakeFest '25 more times than I want to admit. Selling tickets felt like hitting a brick wall. I had come up against so much rejection that the whole thing started to feel impossible. In the end I moved the event indoors because I knew I couldn't mentally do the outdoor risks again. The weather was the big one, and the costs were another. The stress just kept building and I was no longer the brave, bold Nicola. I was broken, mentally and physically. I finally reached what everyone had warned me about.

Huge burnout.

I lost my joy. I felt like a failure. I felt like nobody wanted to work with me and that my business was over. So, I told myself I would get through this last event and that would be it. PeakeFest '25 was going to happen, and then I would step back.

I started repeating new beliefs to myself to make it bearable. Everyone hates it. People are sick of seeing it. They don't want to come because of the negativity. One person even told me that and I let that voice drown out everyone else. I thought about removing my name from everything so people wouldn't associate it with me. I settled into the idea that I'd gone too big too soon and that that was the end.

But I never stop trying to give people a frickin' amazing time. So, I kept going with PeakeFest '25. In the final couple of months before the event I started actually looking after myself. I put myself first for the first time in a long time. I took stock of what I loved and what I didn't love in the business. I sat with how low I'd felt and why a doctor had warned me to step back because it wasn't good for me. I love events. I love everything about them. But I had let myself feel so shit that I had lost sight of that.

Giving up would have been the easy way out. I needed to find myself again. I needed to rebuild my confidence and to stop giving a fuck about whether everyone liked me. I needed to put myself first.

I actually took a break the month before the event. Something I never would have dared to do before. I invested too, using £30k of finance to make PeakeFest '25 as good as I could. I went 'all in' on creating an experience.

I got healthier. I lost weight. I started on anti-depressants. All of the actions slowly cleared the fog and started to bring Nicola back.

The massive thing I couldn't see when I was 'in the dark' was how many beautiful people had my back. People bought tickets, sponsored, championed me, and fought for me online. I hadn't stopped being grateful for them, I'd just been so wrapped up in the negatives that I wasn't seeing the positives. When I started focusing on the people who showed up for me, everything began to change.

I had clouded my own mind with shit. Once I cleared that out, I remembered who I was. And that was the beginning of getting my power back.

10 July 2025. PeakeFest '25 Day One.

I was running back and forth to the toilets, heaving. My anxiety and nervous system were reliving the trauma of the last ten months. How the fuck was I supposed to walk on stage and hold a room when I felt like this?

But I did.

I got up there, looked out at a packed room of smiling, happy faces, and remembered why I loved this so much. I opened the event and announced that PeakeFest was no more. That 2026 would be a one-day event with a new name. Something not tied to me.

As the day went on, I started to see the impact. People were loving it. They told me how amazing it was, how brilliant the branding was, how much they loved our mascot Zammy the Zebra, the name, the whole vibe. Everything I had worked so hard to create for what I thought would be a 'send-off' event.

By day two, the Nicola who had walked on stage the day before was gone.

I was back, baby. Because what lights me up most is people and seeing people happy. That's exactly what this event does.

And this time, the universe played a different joke. Last year I had torrential rain. This year? The hottest days of the year. You couldn't write it. The atmosphere was electric, and two months later people are still posting about it. Still talking about it. Still sharing the love.

What I didn't realise at the time was that this wasn't the end. It was the start of my 'Bold as Fuck' comeback.

I launched 2026 tickets and sold 100 in the first few days. Sponsors started coming to me. Ninety people applied to speak. The feedback was incredible. And then, a week later, I made a bold decision. I had been looking through new name ideas for this 'one-day event' and none of them felt right. The boldest, most audacious thing I could do to show I'm not going anywhere, to show I'm not hiding; to show I will no longer play small no matter what people think… was to keep PeakeFest.

So that's exactly what I did.

2026 won't be a cut-back version. It will be bigger. A full two-day event with fringe networking and a closing party. PeakeFest is not going anywhere, and nor am I.

The funny thing is, I wasn't even going to write about PeakeFest in this book. Only last week I said to Nicky, my friend and publisher, that I would try and share my story without mentioning the event, just in case it stirred up more negativity. But as I sat here writing, I thought, fuck that.

PeakeFest is one of the biggest parts of my life and my business. It's what drives me. It's what gives me the fire to keep growing year on year. It's not just about me, it's about helping more people find their people, grow their businesses, stop feeling so bloody lonely, have fun, connect, and be bold as fuck themselves. Why would I hide that?

So, if you're reading this and you've been holding yourself back, here's what I would love for you to take away.

Ask yourself:

- What are you clinging onto that is keeping you small?
- What old beliefs are you ready to let go of, or who are you ready to let go of?
- Who do you need around you to remind you of your power when you forget it?
- What positives could you choose to focus on instead of giving all your energy to the negatives?
- And most importantly, what is your vision? The one that keeps tugging at you even when you try to push it down.

- How bold are you willing to be to make it happen?

Playing safe will keep you stuck. Playing bold will change everything. You don't need permission. You don't need to wait. You don't need to apologise for wanting more. You just need to decide that average isn't for you.

So be bold. Be brave. Take up space. And whatever your version of PeakeFest is, go and make it real.

And more importantly, if you need help please get it. Don't wait. Don't battle through alone. Whether it's friends, mentors, professionals, or your community, reach out. Because being bold as fuck doesn't mean doing it all by yourself.

If you want to come and experience PeakeFest for yourself, I would love to see you there. Head to PeakeFest.co.uk and get your ticket to join me.

Nicola x

Sara Southey

Sara Southey is the founder and co-Director of The Southey Way Ltd that she runs with her daughter. Their Health & Life Skills company is built around one core belief: Your life, Your health, Your way.

A mother, entrepreneur, Personal Trainer and Life & Health Skills coach, Sara draws on her own transformation journey and over a decade of coaching experience to help purpose-led individuals cut through the noise and find their way back to themself.

Through her signature SOS approach, Sara empowers people to sort out the overwhelm, reconnect with what matters and design their own route to a thriving, fulfilling life.

Links

www.thesoutheyway.com

LinkedIn: http://linkedin.com/in/sarasouthey

Instagram: @sara.thesoutheyway

SOS Your Life Book: https://amzn.eu/d/b5MuZ1E

Speak Up! I Can't Hear You!

Your voice is the most precious gift to and for yourself.

When we are born, both the internal and external voices are ours completely. We know nothing about what others expect of us, nothing about societal norms and family expectations. We just feel, choose, and speak our truth with no other agenda than getting our needs met.

As we start to grow, those external influences start to filter into our unconscious minds and the inner voices start to reflect, control, and modify our voice to ensure we are safe and conform to what is expected of us.

The voice you use to speak out **and** those voices that speak to you internally from deep within your soul and your unconscious mind both influence how you choose to show up in your life, how you choose to live and interact with them.

But they are not the only influence.

There are other voices that influence your decisions and actions. Those external influences and expectations from your family and friends, from your community and culture and from the everyday act of living and working in society.

It can feel like a constant juggle to live and speak your truth whilst respectfully balancing those external influences, maintaining harmony between yourself and your needs and the needs of those around you.

Do not rock the boat, do not do anything different, keep on doing what you have always done as that has worked for you so far, so no need to change anything as this is simply fine how it is.

But.

What if doing the 'right' thing keeps everyone but you happy?

What happens to you when:

- You stay quiet when you want to stand out?
- You do what others expect of you when you want to do something different?
- You do what you are told and what you 'should' do instead of doing what everything within you shouts for you to do?

What happens when those external voices and your internal voices contradict each other, and you must decide which one you will act on? What happens when you feel the conflict between the external influence and your internal needs? When you find yourself voicing opinions and saying yes to actions that you don't want to do or that do not make you happy or bring you joy?

And how do you find your voice to say 'no'?

How do you instill inside yourself the importance of listening to your **own** voice to live your truth?

This is the story of exactly that. How my life changed from *hiding my voice* and not ever speaking out; to *finding my voice* and learning who and what I am and how that sounds; to *living my voice* and being authentically me, true to myself running a business that helps others do the same. And how you too, can take back your voice and live your Bold as Fuck life.

Hiding My Voice

As a child, I was an extravert; outspoken, not ever worrying about where life would take me and how the future would look. I loved to sing and dance. I did ballet from two-and-a-half years old, sang at the top of my lungs, and would spend hours outside exploring and having adventures with the stories in my head, feeding my creative voice. It was carefree, happy, and wonderfully exciting, wondering where the next adventure would take me.

Then slowly I started to hear that it was not acceptable to be this free and easy.

At primary school it started: Sit quietly in class I was told, do not ask so many questions. Be quiet and listen, pay attention and you will be given the answers. I learned not to be enthusiastic. I learned not to show my curiosity. I learned not to ask stupid questions.

At home, our four generation Irish catholic household, around the dinner table, would have many and various heated discussions about life, the universe and everything. The heated debates could go on for hours with any point being raised requiring a strong voice and knowledge to back it up. If not, you would get shouted down quickly and told why your opinion was wrong. I learned not to voice my opinion if I couldn't back it up with chapter & verse. I learned that staying quiet meant I felt less stupid, less exposed to criticism. Being quiet was safe.

In my ballet classes I was told that, although talented, I was the wrong shape to take it further so not to bother. I was told ballerinas weren't my shape. I learned that you have to be a certain shape to fit in and I wasn't it.

Moving into secondary school, as a child of an RAF officer, I went to boarding school and the voices got stronger and more opinionated about how I was wrong to be 'me.'

At the medical evaluation, in front of a whole class of girls I was told 'Oh look! You are as round as you are tall' and 'you are too short to weigh that much'. I learned my body was not how it was meant to be. I learned that my height and weight were not acceptable.

When the terms kept passing it was clear that there were certain groups of girls: the cool girls, the clever girls, the dramatic girls, the geeky girls. There were unspoken rules to gain admittance to these groups. I learned that I did not know the rules. I learned I did not fit into any of the groups even though I desperately wanted to.

I learned that if I modified my behavior and my actions, swallowed my natural excitement and enthusiasm for life, that I would be more palatable and acceptable to those around me. Be it my peer group, teachers, family, or other people of influence in my life.

And so, my voice and I gradually went into hiding.

I learned to play the game. To swallow my realness and show only what was acceptable to the world. When my careers teacher told me not to bother going to university as I would never make anything of myself, my internal feistiness rebelled and I went anyway but 6 months later when I realised academia really was not for me and I was failing the course already, so I quit. And without telling my parents, I quietly got myself a job. With a huge sense of failure, I took this as a sign that my careers teacher must have been correct. I learned that other people's opinions of me must be right. That I should listen to and do as they say. Otherwise, I will fail again!

And so, hiding my voice became my norm.

Every job I applied for, post uni failure, I expected to be found out that I was a failure. In the first 5 years of working I was made redundant 4 times. I learned that I was a failure!

After an early adventurous start into romance, I settled into a five-and-a-half-year relationship where I was compliant and not outspoken. It ended when it became obviously controlling and aggressive. I learned I did not make great choices with my partners. I learned I was not worth the emotional effort.

The years went on. Outwardly I was happy, had fun and loved a party. I learned that when I was this person, nobody asked if I was OK. So I did not have to lie or tell the truth.

I learned if I made everyone around me happy, then there was never any conflict and life would be ok.

And then, eventually, I could not hide any more.

Finding my voice

Fast forward a few years: Living in America where my husband had been working for five years and where, due to the visas, I had not been allowed to work. I had several months' worth of undiagnosed depression, where I spent hours on my own watching shit daytime TV with tears streaming down my face, wondering who I was and what I was doing here. Because I had learned to hide my voice, I said nothing. I told nobody. It was around this time we decided it was the perfect time to have children.

Then, I was thirty years old with two kids, living in a beautiful part of New Jersey. With a lovely husband who was away a lot and surrounded by many people living and working in a new culture that is so different to the culture I had learned to survive in.

I was miserable as sin, again I felt like I was failing at life.

From the outside it looked like I had everything: A beautiful house, a great husband, two beautiful children and enough money coming in that we could live life very comfortably. Inside? I was so unhappy, in a country that looked like where I had grown up but was culturally different. Conforming to new expectations and an identity of me as a wife and mother whilst inside the discontent was starting to solidify into a driving purpose to change my life. The first step I took was when we had the opportunity to stay in America. We had to make a choice and when asked I realised that I had to state my opinion, or nothing was going to change for the foreseeable future. I dug deep and found a scrap of my voice. I said that I wanted to go home. Once I said it once, the need to go home grew inside me. It was impossible to ignore. Which made it easier to keep saying I want to go home. I learned that when the pain is great enough, I can voice my opinion. I learned that once I said it once, it was much easier to say it again. I learned that once I put my thoughts out into the real world that they can be heard and cannot be taken back.

We returned home to the UK. As we had sold our house before moving to America, we had nowhere to live. So, we moved in with my parents into our four-generation house. As I mentioned previously, it was a feisty opinionated environment. And it was not long before my husband and my mother fell out with each other, big time! We managed five days in the family home before things came to a head. The pain of the conflict was so great that I had to choose between staying with the kids whilst my husband left or leaving with my husband and kids. Again, I found my voice and chose it. The next day, we moved out and stayed with friends. It was six weeks before we found our home and six months before my mother and I talked again. I learned that sometimes you **must** use your voice. I learned when I was backed into a corner, any decision I voice that gets me out of a painful place is an effective use of my voice.

Once we had our own home and moved in, my husband and I discussed work and kids. We investigated our options. As my husband was the main wage earner it was obvious that he had to continue working. Then the question was whether I stayed at home to bring up the kids or whether I went back to work. My gut said to go back to work. Not being a particularly broody mother and not much enjoying the baby stage I could have emotionally and physically handled being a working mother. However, when we looked at jobs and the cost of childcare, practicality won. I did not strongly voice my gut instinct. I went with the practical and financially beneficial option which was for me to stay at home and bring up the kids.

For the next ten years I did the best job I could to bring up our children. Externally all looked well. Internally I was miserable. I was so unhappy, I felt trapped in a life I didn't want to live, I felt a failure each and every time I didn't enjoy the school gate chat or the creation of book day fancy dress. I failed each time I bought rather than baked for the school fetes. I told nobody how bad it was. How sometimes I fantasised about dropping the kids off at school and driving off to never return! And that made me feel even worse. Because I loved my family with my whole being. But I did not love the life I was living.

I learned that listening to my gut and speaking my truth no matter how uncomfortable at the time, when we decided whether I would get a job and be employed or stay home would have been so much less painful than the life I was currently living. I learned that rather than continue how I was going and risk blowing up my life in a drastic and dramatic fashion, I could learn to use my voice for myself. To express how I felt and what I wanted. I vowed to practice in the smallest steps I could find until that felt natural, then take another slightly bigger step and practice that until it felt natural.

For the next few years as the kids went through primary and then secondary school, I practiced. I practiced saying no when I meant no. I practiced listening to my gut and actioning what it told me. I practiced learning from what did not feel right and finding my way of doing things that sat well with me. I practiced exploring who I was deep down in my soul and bringing that person out into the light more. I practiced stretching myself out of my comfort zone through physical challenges, which in turn showed me how much strength and resilience I already had inside that I had not been using for myself. I practiced putting myself first at the top of my to-do list so that my bucket could be filled up with soul-feeding energy.

The more I practiced, the more grounded in myself I felt. The more grounded I felt, the surer I became of my voice and expressing what I wanted. The more I used my voice, the happier I felt. The happier I felt in myself the more I was able to give to my family, my friends and then through the company I set up to help others with their version of this process.

Finally, I was using my voice. Using it how I wanted to use it. Using it according to my own rules and to meet my own needs. And nothing drastic happened as a result. My family and friends still love me. In fact, relationships became clearer and more based on honesty and clarity and less about trying to second guess what the 'right' thing to do would be. Using my voice was liberating, empowering and enabled me to spread those ripples of hope, happiness and purpose out into the world.

Living my voice

Finding my voice has opened so many opportunities for me. I rediscovered that little girl who loved to sing and dance. The little girl that created stories and had adventures. That little girl who did not think about what she 'should' do. The little girl that was curious, vibrant, and alive. Curious about the world and the people in it. Finding out about different people and their stories. That little girl is now me, aged fifty-four and aging with fun and happiness in my life.

Now I live my voice.

I never ignore my gut instincts. I always ask 'why?' When something does not feel right. I do not do anything just because it is expected of me. I always speak my truth. I am 100% committed to living my best life possible. And that starts with me living my voice and speaking my truths. Here are a few key truths I use to remind me regularly when I get challenged.

- Adulting is overrated - only do it when you must
- The word 'should' is a red flag that is always a learning opportunity - why should I?
- Never ignore a strong gut reaction - if you do it often does not work out for the best
- We only have one life so do not live someone else's - find what YOUR best life looks like and then live the crap out of it
- Do it your way - learn what you can from others and then find the way that works for you!

These truths are now so ingrained in my soul that they permeate through everything I do, at home, with family and friends and through our work at The Southey Way. So called because we did it our way and we help you do it your way.

Having been running The Southey Way since 2016, I have worked with many clients helping them find their way through to their best life. And now I have written it down so that you too can find your way through this crazy journey called life. My book, SOS Your Life, will guide you through exploring who you are and what you want and need out of your life and how you can achieve that throughout your life.

There are only two certainties in this journey called life. At the start, when you are born and at the very end when you die. The rest of the journey YOU get to choose which routes you take. Living your best life IS possible. You do not have to blow up your whole life to live it either. You just need to take back your voice and choose.

Tell me, where will you go?

If you are not sure where you want to go or how you will get there, here's a small step you could take to start you on your journey; buy SOS Your Life.

Shane Evans

Shane Evans is a coach, trainer and speaker who helps people take back the wheel and lead themselves with purpose, courage and impact. After two decades in leadership and HR, he founded Shane Evans Coaching to work with professionals, leaders and teams across the UK. Known as The Self-Leadership Guy, Shane blends straight talk with humour and heart to step out of drifting and into driving. When he's not coaching, you'll find him with his family, at a gig, or talking tattoos and football.

Links

- Website: www.secoach.co.uk
- LinkedIn: linkedin.com/in/shanecoach
- Facebook: facebook.com/secoach.co.uk
- Threads: threads.com/@secoach.co.uk
- Book: Be Your Own Leader – Available on Amazon

Drifting to Driving

Introduction: Who I Am and Why This Matters

If you'd met me twenty years ago, you might have thought I had it sorted. On the surface, it looked like I was driving my own life. A steady career, decent salary, family life, the suit and tie. I ticked all the boxes that were supposed to mean 'success.'

But here's the thing: ticking boxes doesn't always mean you're in the driver's seat. Sometimes it just means you've let someone else write the map.

My name's Shane Evans, and these days I'm known as *The Self-Leadership Guy*. I coach professionals, leaders and teams across the UK, I work with the high performers who are lost, the misfits, the grafters, and the overlooked. The people who've been underestimated or boxed in but know deep down they're capable of more. I help them take control of the steering wheel of their lives.

But I didn't land here by accident. In fact, my career started nowhere near HR. It started in the kitchen.

Back in the 90s, I was a chef on the London circuit. It was everything I wanted at the time: the buzz, the intensity, the pace and excitement. It was brutal but exhilarating. The hours were long, the pressure relentless, but that's what I thought 'making it' looked like. After a while, though, the glamour wore thin. I was burnt out. The hours that once fuelled me started to grind me down. I knew I couldn't live at that pace forever.

So I pivoted. I went into food manufacturing... cooking at scale. At first it was just a job, but I quickly found myself promoted into leadership roles. Suddenly I wasn't just cooking; I was managing people, driving operations, handling health and safety, pushing continuous improvement. I got thrown into the deep end of cultural change programmes, and before long I was standing in a training room, teaching and facilitating groups of people to get to grips with the values and beliefs of an organisation.

And that's when it clicked. This kind of work - helping people understand themselves, connect with others and grow, it felt natural. Everything I'd ever loved about work revolved around people. Maybe, just maybe, a career in HR was the way forward.

So, I made the leap. Over the next two decades, I built a career in HR, specialising in Learning and Development and leadership development, largely in manufacturing - a tough environment where you learnt fast or got left behind. I saw the best and worst of leadership. I saw talented people overlooked because they were quiet and louder people promoted because they played the game. I saw myself, ambitious, capable, but too often drifting.

Drifting doesn't feel dangerous at first. It feels safe. You hit the marks, collect the salary and keep everyone happy. But drifting costs you years. It steals energy, clarity and joy. And the harsh truth is this: nobody rescues you. The only person who can grab the wheel is you.

That realisation changed everything. Slowly at first, then more boldly, I began to take back the wheel. I lost four stone through daily discipline - no hacks, no quick fixes, just consistent effort. I started showing up online as myself, not the polished HR version I thought people expected. I leaned into coaching, which had always been the part of HR I loved most: helping people grow, find confidence, and back themselves. Eventually, I left the corporate ladder behind and built a coaching business on my own terms.

The boldest move wasn't starting a business, or even leaving a secure job. It was admitting, honestly, that I'd been drifting and deciding to take the wheel. That moment of self-leadership changed everything.

This chapter is about that shift, from drifting to driving and the framework I now use with my clients: the four pillars of self-leadership.

Spotting the Drift

Drifting is sneaky. It doesn't happen in one dramatic moment, it creeps in quietly. One day you're fired up about work, pushing for something that matters. The next, you're on autopilot. You still look busy, you still hit deadlines, but the spark has gone.

The thing with drifting is that it feels safe. It doesn't demand anything of you beyond showing up and going through the motions. And at first it's not uncomfortable. You can coast for months, even years, without really noticing. Until one day you realise you've gone miles off track.

So what does drifting look like in real life?

- **Energy without direction.** You're working hard, but you're not sure what for. The hours are there, the effort is there, but you don't feel progress.

- **Vague answers.** When someone asks, 'What's next for you?' and you either change the subject or reel off something that doesn't excite you.

- **Default mode.** Saying yes to projects you don't care about, just because you can do them or it's easier than saying no.

- **Waiting.** For permission, for recognition, for the perfect time. Deep down, you know it's not coming.

I've drifted more times than I'd like to admit. One memory still sticks. I was in a leadership meeting, surrounded by senior managers arguing over budgets and policies. Everyone seemed desperate to win the point, to prove their importance. I remember sitting there, watching the theatre of it all, and thinking: *I don't even want the job they're fighting for.*

That thought hit hard. I'd been working for years to climb the ladder. And there I was, looking at the rung above me, realising I didn't want it. I wasn't excited, I wasn't proud, I was just… flat. That's drift.

Another time, it was more personal. I looked in the mirror one morning and barely recognised myself. Tired, carrying too much weight, always stressed. I was a dad to three boys and I knew they were watching me, learning from how I lived, not just what I said and the example I was setting? Drift again. That moment was painful, but it was also a turning point. It made me ask: *Is this who I want to be?*

Drifting doesn't only happen at work. I see it in coaching clients who come to me with stories like:

- 'I fell into this career and I've just kept going.'
- 'I was overlooked for promotion again, but I'm not sure why.'
- 'I don't hate my job, but I don't love it either. I'm just... here.'

They're smart, capable, hardworking people. But they've stopped steering.

The real danger of drifting is that it normalises itself. You tell yourself it's fine, that everyone feels this way. You settle and slowly, you shrink.

But here's the uncomfortable truth: nobody pulls you out of the drift. You can get encouragement, support, even coaching. But ultimately, you're the only one who can grab the wheel.

The good news is it doesn't take a dramatic leap to break the drift. It takes awareness. Simply admitting to yourself 'I've been coasting,' is a bold move in itself. Because once you see it, you can't unsee it. You've created a gap between where you are and where you could be and that gap is the start of change.

Think about it: have you ever driven a car and realised you'd zoned out for the last ten minutes? You didn't crash, you stayed on the road, but you can't really remember the journey. That's drifting and just like on the road, the moment you notice, you sit up straighter, put your hands back firmly on the wheel and start driving again.

That's where self-leadership comes in. It's the shift from being a passenger in your own life to being the driver. For me it comes down to four simple but powerful pillars: self-awareness, mindset, action and impact. Together, they're the system that keeps you moving with intention, even when life throws detours and potholes your way.

Pillar 1: Self-Awareness - See the Patterns, Own the Story

You can't drive with your eyes shut. Self-awareness is about switching the headlights on so you can see where you are, what habits keep pulling you off track, and what story you're telling yourself.

For me, one big pattern was hiding. Early in my HR career, I played 'corporate Shane.' Smart shirt, careful language, tattoos covered. Outwardly confident, inwardly cautious. I told people to bring their whole selves to work while leaving parts of mine out of sight. At the time I thought it was professional - really, it was fear (and slightly hypocritical) and once I saw that contradiction, I couldn't unsee it.

Self-awareness also showed up in my health. I'd ignored the obvious: poor habits, low energy, and I had put on too much weight. I told myself I was too busy. The truth was I didn't want to face how far I'd drifted. Looking in the mirror one morning was brutal, but that awareness was the spark that got me moving again.

I see the same in clients. One leader blamed his team for missed deadlines until he realised his own late-night emails and stress were setting the tone. He wasn't a bad leader; just an unaware one. Once he spotted the pattern, we could change it.

Building self-awareness isn't complicated. Journal for five minutes:

'Where did I drift today? Where did I drive?' Ask people you trust 'What's it like to be on the other side of me?' Notice what your body tells you before your brain does.

Self-awareness isn't about over-analysing every flaw. It's about honesty and should be done with kindness. Once you own your story, you can start to write a new one.

Pillar 2: Mindset – Choose the Frame that Serves You

If self-awareness is switching the headlights on, mindset is deciding where you'll steer. Drift mode says, *this is just how it is*. Driving says, *what can I do with this?*

When I left the security of corporate life, fear was loud. No guaranteed money coming in, three kids and a mortgage. My head was full of reasons to play safe. But I chose a different frame. *What if this is the chance to build something that actually fits me and fulfils my purpose*? That thought didn't remove the risk, but it shifted the energy. Instead of clinging to safety, I leaned into possibility.

That's the power of mindset. It reframes obstacles into options. It doesn't mean pretending things are perfect - that's toxic positivity. It means recognising reality and then choosing a frame that helps, not hinders.

I've seen this with clients too. One came to me convinced they weren't 'leadership material.' They'd been overlooked for promotion (again) and the story in their head was, *I'm just not cut out for it*. Together, we flipped the frame. Instead of asking, 'Why not me?' we asked, 'What would it take for me to show up like a leader today?' That one shift changed how they spoke in meetings, how they set boundaries, and how others saw them. Within months, they were leading projects they'd never imagined stepping into.

Mindset is your satnav. If it's set to 'victim' you'll circle the same roads forever. Set it to 'accountable' and new routes open up.

Here are two questions that help me reset when drift creeps in:

- 'Am I reacting, or am I driving?'
- 'What frame would serve me better right now?'

Mindset doesn't fix everything but without it, nothing shifts. The way you choose to see a situation often decides whether you stall or move forward.

Pillar 3: Action -Small, Consistent, Accountable Steps

Driving isn't one big yank of the wheel. It's a series of small adjustments that keep you on the road. That's what action in self-leadership looks like; not a single heroic leap, but steady, deliberate steps that add up over time.

When I lost four stone, people asked me what the 'secret' was. There wasn't one. It wasn't a fad diet. It was daily discipline, eating less and moving more. Saying no to old habits. Most days it felt boring, but stacked together, those choices created momentum.

Business worked the same way. I didn't grow an audience by landing one viral post. It happened because I showed up every day on LinkedIn and Facebook, sharing thoughts even when engagement was low. Action beats overthinking. Drift breaks the moment you move.

I've seen clients transform through action too. One was paralysed by indecision about a career change. They'd analysed every option, made endless pros and cons lists, but stayed stuck. I asked them to choose one small step that week; just one conversation with someone in their desired field. That chat led to another, then another, and within months they'd built the confidence and network to land a new role. The big leap came, but only after the small steps.

Here's the truth: motivation is overrated. It comes and goes. Action builds momentum and momentum fuels motivation. The trick is to shrink things down until doing them feels impossible to avoid. Want to get fitter? Start with a ten-minute walk. Want to speak up more at work? Ask one question in the next meeting. Want to change your career? Send a message to someone who's already where you want to be.

Don't keep it to yourself. Accountability changes everything. Tell a friend, a colleague, a coach. Once the commitment is spoken, drift gets harder to hide in.

So if you want to move from drifting to driving, stop waiting for the perfect plan. Choose one bold step this week. Take it. Then take another. It's that simple and that hard.

Pillar 4: Impact- Show Up in a Way That Lifts Others

Driving isn't just about you. You're sharing the road. The way you drive affects everyone around you whether you realise it or not.

When I worked in manufacturing leadership and I came in stressed and distracted, the whole team felt it. Productivity dipped, tempers flared, mistakes crept in. But on the days I showed up calm, clear and intentional, it lifted the room. The same meetings ran smoother, the same targets felt lighter. My behaviour was the thermostat.

At home, it's even more obvious. My boys don't just listen to what I say - they watch how I live. They see how I handle setbacks, how I speak to my amazing wife and how I react when things go wrong. That's what shapes them. When I'm drifting, they notice.

Impact is about the ripple effect, your choices, your mindset, and your energy which spill outwards. If you're coasting your team, your family and your friends feel it. If you're driving, they feel that too. And here's the beauty: when you lead yourself well, you give permission for others to do the same.

One client came to me burned out, convinced they had nothing left to give. Through working together, they started leading themselves better. Setting boundaries, making time for rest and being honest about what they wanted. Within months, not only were they thriving, but their team noticed too. Morale lifted, and performance improved. One person's shift created a ripple across a whole department.

So how do you check your impact? End each week by asking one simple question: 'Did my energy lift or drain the people around me?' If the answer's drain, don't beat yourself up, just choose one tweak for next week. Maybe it's switching off earlier. Maybe it's saying no to one more meeting. Maybe it's showing a little more appreciation. Small shifts in how you show up can have massive ripples.

In the end, leadership isn't about the title on your business card, it's about the impact you leave behind. Another way to look at this is to think about your retirement party in the future, visualise who you want to be there and what you want them to say about you? Now go and act that way every day.

The Bold Move

When people hear 'bold,' they often picture big leaps. Maybe slapping your boss and quitting your job in a movie-style fashion, moving countries or starting a business on a whim. Yes, sometimes bold looks like that but for me? The boldest move I've ever made wasn't flashy it was quieter.

It was admitting, in the middle of a secure career, with responsibilities and a family to provide for, that I was drifting again. On the outside, things looked fine. I had status, stability and a clear path forward. But inside, I knew I wasn't steering anymore. I was letting other people's expectations decide the route.

The moment I owned that, I had a choice: carry on drifting, or take the wheel. Taking the wheel meant risk. It meant saying no to opportunities that didn't fit. It meant showing up online as myself, tattoos and all. It meant building a business that reflected my values rather than someone else's. It isn't always easy, but it is real.

That's the truth about boldness. Sometimes it's loud, but often it's quiet. It's not always about burning bridges, it's about looking yourself in the mirror and saying, *I'm done drifting*. That decision changes everything.

Conclusion and Call to Action

Life will always throw detours. You can't control every pothole, storm or traffic jam. But you can always choose how you drive.

Drifting is normal. Staying there is optional.

So, here's your challenge. Pick one area of your life or career where you've been drifting. Write down one bold step you'll take in the next 24 hours to move it forward. Then do it. Don't wait for permission. Bold doesn't wait.

Because at the end of the day, nobody else can grab the wheel for you. It's your turn to drive.

Thanks for reading, I wish you every success moving Onward and Forward.

Sharon Banham

Sharon Banham is an intuitive, dynamic hypnotherapist and founder of *Calm Directions*. She helps women over 40 reconnect with themselves as life roles shift, guiding them to uncover their inner strength, self-worth, and purpose. Drawing on her background in mental-health practice and deep subconscious work, Sharon combines science, intuition, and compassion to create lasting transformation. Her philosophy is simple: *I am the guide, you are the key*. She works online and from her peaceful therapy space in Norfolk, helping clients rediscover calm, confidence, and clarity.

www.calmdirections.co.uk

Unlock the Courage to be Seen

I'm here in this book because I was both craving and fearing visibility.

I've been a hypnotherapist since 2021, always fitting it in around an employed role, keeping things small, relying on word of mouth and making a pretty poor effort on social media. I decided I wanted to reach a wider audience and took action to learn how to do that. I worked with a couple of different coaches, joined several business groups, signed up for challenges (some free, most not) and while I gained a lot from all of this - nothing truly shifted.

Last year, I had major FOMO (Fear Of Missing Out) when I saw posts about PeakeFest, a festival inspired business event centered around visibility, connection and implementation. Several friends were going, and I wasn't able to attend. As soon as the early bird sales for this year went up, I was in.

A couple of months before the event, Nicola put up a visibility package offer, and I jumped in on impulse. This, I thought, would force me to face my introvert fears and finally step out of those comfort zones. A spot in this book was part of the package, but I had no idea what I could possibly write about. As usual, I was winging it.

Fast forward to a week before PeakeFest and I was bricking it. I was even trying to decide whether my excuse for not attending would be 'having Covid' or 'some other crisis.' But my FOMO pushed me forward, and I went. I participated in all of my visibility challenges, made new friends, listened to incredible talks, and generally had a blast.

And now I'm here, writing a chapter for a book about being *bold*. As a quiet introvert, what the hell do I have to say about being bold?

Here's what I've learned: being bold isn't about being loud, boisterous, or in-your-face. It's about pushing through fears. It's about stepping up even though part of you is feeling like you don't belong here. It's about taking action, despite the imposter syndrome; and when you do that, something powerful happens and you prove to yourself that you can. You get feedback, connection, validation. That's what being bold really is.

So, this chapter is about how to step outside those comfort zones and move beyond the subconscious blocks, limiting beliefs, imposter syndrome, or worthiness wounds that keep us playing small.

In my hypnotherapy practice, I've found myself working with many women who, like me, are Gen X. Women moving through their 40s, 50s, and beyond; women who feel frustrated, unfulfilled, or invisible.

Some are mothers adjusting to children becoming young adults, no longer needed for late-night lift rescues or job and university applications. Others have built successful careers, only to discover that 'success' feels strangely hollow. Somewhere along the way, they lost themselves. They became versions of who they thought they *should* be - reshaping how they look, sound, even walk, anything that helped them fit the mould society required.

And then comes the kicker: society tells us our worth diminishes with age. As if the appearance of a few grey hairs means we fade into irrelevance too.

These women arrive in my chair craving self-worth, self-love, and fighting that lost sense of self. They're tired of fading into the background, but afraid to be seen. They want to be bold, but visibility feels like the scariest thing of all.

Why Visibility Feels So Hard

Here's the thing nobody tells you: if visibility feels hard, it's not because you're weak, lazy, or not cut out for business. It's because your brain is doing its job.

Our subconscious is wired to keep us safe, not successful. Thousands of years ago, standing out could mean rejection, and rejection could mean danger. Fast forward to today, and your subconscious still hasn't updated the software. Hitting 'publish' on a post, introducing yourself at an event, or speaking up in a meeting? Your brain treats it like stepping into the lion's den.

That's why visibility often triggers the body's threat response: racing heart, sweaty palms, the voice in your head shouting, 'Don't do it - you'll make a fool of yourself.' It's not that you're broken. It's just old programming.

And that programming is sneaky. It drives self-sabotaging behaviours designed to keep you safe.

The Subconscious Patterns That Keep Us Small

1. **Fear of Judgment**

   Did you grow up hearing, *'Don't do that! What will the neighbours think?'* Or perhaps your efforts at school were met with criticism instead of encouragement. The subconscious learned: people are watching, and judgment hurts. So as adults, we avoid situations where we might be judged.

2. **Imposter Syndrome**

   That sinking feeling that you're not good enough, not qualified enough, not experienced enough. Everyone else knows more. One day, someone will find you out. So you hold back from opportunities that are perfect for you.

3. **The Worthiness Wound**

   This is the deep-rooted belief that you're not enough - not smart enough, not polished enough, not worthy enough. Often born from early experiences of being overlooked or dismissed, it's reinforced by years of putting others first.

   In business, this shows up as:

   - Holding back your story because you fear it's 'not good enough.'

   - Under-pricing your services or hesitating to sell.

   - Constantly comparing yourself to others and coming up short.

The shift?

Worthiness isn't something you earn, it's something you claim. Bold visibility begins the moment you stop waiting to feel worthy and instead decide:

I belong here, exactly as I am.

The Visibility Hangover

You finally share that vulnerable post, speak on a panel, or pitch to a dream client. In the moment, it feels amazing. The next day? Doubt creeps in. You replay every word, cringe at imagined mistakes, and wonder if everyone thought you were ridiculous. That emotional high dips into a low of self-questioning.

This happens because visibility stretches your nervous system. Afterwards, the subconscious rushes to drag you back to safety, saying *'Let's not do that again.'*

But here's the truth: a visibility hangover isn't failure. It's growth. Each time you step out again, the hangovers get shorter until visibility feels natural instead of nerve-wracking.

A Tool For Bold Moments

Here's a simple exercise you can use whenever visibility feels terrifying:

1. **Imagine the fear.**
   Close your eyes and picture the situation: posting online, speaking up in a meeting, walking into a room. Notice the feelings. Don't judge them.

2. **Create your anchor.**

    Place your hand on your heart or stomach. Breathe slowly and say:

    I am calm. I am safe. I am in control.

    Repeat three times.

3. **Reframe the story.**

    Still holding the anchor, imagine yourself taking the action - calm, grounded, even at ease. Let your body learn what safe visibility feels like.

4. **Use it in real life.**

    Next time fear rises, use the anchor. Then take the step.

Confidence Comes After Action

We often think we need confidence before we act. We wait until we feel ready. But waiting is a trap. The longer you wait, the louder the inner critic becomes.

Confidence doesn't come first. Action does.
The moment you take the step - *that's* when confidence grows.

This is why I showed up at PeakeFest even though every part of me wanted to shrink and hide. My inner critic had plenty to say, but honestly? These days it just sounds a bit lame.

That's the heart of bold visibility. It isn't about volume. It isn't about being the loudest in the room. It's about choosing to step forward even with the voice of doubt in your ear. It's about claiming your worth and proving to yourself that you can.

That's why I'm writing this chapter now. To remind you: you don't have to wait until you feel fearless. You just have to decide to show up.

So, here's my invitation: the next time you feel that familiar fear rising, use the anchor. Breathe. Say the words: *I am calm. I am safe. I am in control.* Then take the step. Post the thing. Say the words. Walk into the room.

You don't have to roar to be bold. You just have to show up.

In my work as a hypnotherapist, I always say: *I am the guide - you are the key.*

That means I don't 'fix' people. I don't wave a magic wand and make their fears, blocks, or doubts vanish. What I do is guide them to unlock the doors they've already been holding the keys to all along.

When it comes to visibility, this philosophy matters. If I simply pushed someone onto a stage or handed them a script for a video, that moment of courage might be a one-off. They'd survive it, maybe even feel proud, but the next time fear showed up, they'd be back at square one.

Real, lasting boldness comes from within. It comes from shifting the subconscious patterns that whisper *'you're not enough'* or *'you'll be judged'* into something truer, kinder, and more powerful.

One of my clients, I'll call her Kate, came to me after years of drifting in her corporate role. She was brilliant at her job, but when it came to stepping into the spotlight, she'd freeze and this was really holding her back. In our sessions, what came up wasn't just fear of speaking - it was a lifetime of being told to 'keep quiet' and 'not show off.' Her subconscious had built the belief that visibility equals arrogance. Once we worked through that, she began putting herself forward for projects, sharing her ideas with clarity and confidence. Within months, she was asked to speak at a company-wide event and she said 'yes' without hesitation, and has since quit her job and opened her own consultancy business.

The key wasn't me giving her confidence. The key was her rediscovering that she already had something worth sharing.

Another client, let's call her Julie, was a mother of three who felt invisible in every sense. Her children were becoming independent, she had walked away from a corporate role to raise her family, and she confessed to feeling like she'd 'disappeared.' In our work together, she uncovered a deep worthiness wound from childhood, years of being compared to a 'golden sibling.' Once she saw that old pattern for what it was, everything shifted. She started painting again, something she'd abandoned decades earlier, and eventually she opened a small online shop selling her work. For her, visibility wasn't about social media likes, it was about reclaiming a voice, a presence and a gift she thought she'd lost forever.

That's why I believe visibility isn't about forcing yourself into the spotlight. It's about finding your way back to the truth of who you are, and then letting that truth be seen.

When you realise you already hold the key, being bold doesn't feel like a performance. It feels like coming home.

Reclaiming Visibility as Self-Leadership

So often, visibility gets reduced to a marketing strategy. Post three times a week. Show up on video. Share your wins. And while those tactics have their place, they miss the deeper truth.

Visibility is leadership.

Every time you choose to show up authentically, you send a message, not just about your business, but about what's possible. You give others permission to step forward too.

I've seen this ripple effect again and again. A client finally shared her story online, and her inbox filled with messages from other women saying, *'That's exactly how I feel, thank you for sharing.'* Another client spoke at a charity event. When she came to me this felt so far out of her comfort zone, but afterwards a young woman approached her and said, *'You've inspired me to start my own business!'*

This is what happens when we shift visibility from being about *us* to being about *service*. When you show the world who you truly are, you're not just marketing. You're modelling courage. You're creating space for others to do the same. That's why visibility matters.

So here's my call to you: stop waiting for confidence. Stop waiting for the perfect moment, the polished post, the 'right' words.

Bold visibility doesn't start with perfection. It starts with one choice - the choice to show up.

Maybe that means hitting 'publish' on a post you've been sitting on for weeks. Maybe it means introducing yourself at a networking event instead of lingering at the back. Maybe it's as simple as telling your story, out loud, to someone who needs to hear it.

Whatever it looks like for you, choose one act of brave visibility this week, and commit to it.

And when the fear rises, as it will, use the anchor:
Hand to heart. Slow breath. 'I am calm. I am safe. I am in control.'

Because boldness isn't about being loud. It's about showing up anyway. And you, right now, already hold the key.

I will leave you with my favourite technique to gain a boost of confidence in the moments before you have to do something visible:

As you're standing there, imagine that stood just in front of you, there is a confident version of you, see everything you can about this version of yourself, look how she stands, her posture, the smile on her face and in her eyes, imagine how confident she is feeling right now and then magnify it 10 times, 20 times, 100 times more! And then you simply take a slow deep breath in and at the same time step into that version, breathe her in and feel her confidence flood through you, lifting you, filling you with that same confidence. Practice this anytime you can, and you'll find it gets easier and more effective every time. When your comfortable with it – you can even do it while you're stood talking to someone, and all they'll see is you shift your position slightly, meanwhile you feel like you've had a surge of confidence flow through every nerve in your body!

I began this journey craving and fearing visibility in equal measure. What I've learned is that boldness isn't something you build — it's something you remember. When you meet yourself fully and step into your own light, you don't just become visible to the world — you become visible to yourself. And that changes everything.

So take the step. Speak the truth. Share the story. Not because you're fearless, but because you're ready to lead yourself home. The world doesn't need perfect voices, it needs real ones. And yours, exactly as it is, can carry a powerful message.

WORK WITH NICOLA

If reading these stories lights something up in you, if it reminds you that you have more to say and more to give, then I want you to know that there is space for you in my world. You have a bold voice, a powerful story, and a level of impact that goes far beyond what you can see right now. You can be visible in a way that feels good, you can stand on stages, you can grow communities, you can lead, and you can do it without shrinking or pretending.

That is the work I do. I help people own who they are, speak with confidence, and use their bold voice to build something unforgettable. Whether it is inside my communities or on my stages, you are always welcome to step into this bold as F*ck world with me, a world built for people who are ready to rise, ready to be seen, and ready to back themselves fully.

You are bold, you are capable, and you can achieve anything you decide to go after. Let this book be your reminder that there is so much more waiting for you, and you do not have to do any of it alone.

PEAKEFEST

NICOLA PEAKE

www.ingramcontent.com/pod-product-compliance
Lightning Source LLC
Chambersburg PA
CBHW031406040426
42444CB00005B/438